I0753541

W·G·Reeve

ANNALS

OF THE

FIRST AFRICAN CHURCH,

IN

THE UNITED STATES OF AMERICA,

NOW STYLED

The African Episcopal Church of St. Thomas,

PHILADELPHIA,

IN ITS CONNECTION WITH THE EARLY STRUGGLES OF THE COLORED PEOPLE TO IMPROVE THEIR CONDITION, WITH THE CO-OPERATION OF THE FRIENDS, AND OTHER PHILANTHROPISTS; PARTLY DERIVED FROM THE MINUTES OF A BENEFICIAL SOCIETY, ESTABLISHED BY ABSALOM JONES, RICHARD ALLEN AND OTHERS, IN 1787, AND PARTLY FROM THE MINUTES OF THE AFORESAID CHURCH,

By the REV. WM. DOUGLASS,

RECTOR.

PHILADELPHIA:
KING & BAIRD, PRINTERS, No. 607 SANSOM STREET.
1862.

CONTENTS.

PREFACE.

THAT separate and distinct churches for colored people are now established here, and in different parts of the country, is a fact, the propriety of which the subscriber has considered useless to discuss. It is much more in accordance with his natural promptings, to identify himself with the praiseworthy deeds of his predecessors—to travel back to those events with which they were intimately connected, and which transpired before he was born, simply addressing himself to the whole train of those past occurrences, which, under a wise and inscrutable Providence have led to results of incalculable good,—than to be hypercritical, in regard to what may now appear to have been a mistaken policy on their part. Some time ago, he had the privilege of conversing with many of the old members—all now gone to their final account—who had a vivid recollection of the laying of the corner stone of St. Thomas' Church. He has often listened with intense interest to their recital of the toils and labors, trials and difficulties which they encountered, both previous and subsequent to the erection of the building. He often indulged the wish, that he possessed in some regular form, the facts which they related to him with so much gusto. Looking over the old records of the Church a few years ago, the facts aforesaid, unexpectedly presented themselves; and as the said wish is participated in by many of the present members of the Church, he now offers them to public view, shaped, he hopes, in an acceptable, if not in the best possible form. And should the interest in reading the following pages, be equal to the pleasure had in arranging the matter therein contained, the undersigned will be truly happy.

W. D.

INTRODUCTION.

Seventy-five years ago, no church edifice could be found throughout the whole country, owned and controlled exclusively by persons of color. The religiously disposed among them were then under the necessity of worshipping in churches belonging to their white brethren. As Methodism addressed itself chiefly to the feelings and affections,—which are always strongest among undisciplined minds,—the great majority gave their adherence to that system. Another cause of the success of this denomination in gathering to their folds more of the colored population than any other, may be ascribed to their Itinerancy. This class of ministers, at the time referred to, made no pretensions to literary qualifications, and being despised and persecuted as religious enthusiasts, their sympathies naturally turned towards the lowly, who, like themselves, were of small estimate in the sight of worldly greatness. In those days that denomination of christians could lay claim to but one house of worship in Philadelphia. This is situated in Fourth Street below Vine, and is known by the title of St. George's Church. Here it was that the larger portion of the colored population of the city assembled from time to time on occasions of public worship.

Here, they, in common with others, gave vent to their devotional feelings without let or hindrance. They had comfortable seats on the lower floor of that building to which there were no objections made, until the increasing numbers of the congregation, afforded a plea on the part of those invested with power, for desiring their removal to the gallery. But as they had contributed their mites towards paying for the building in which all the seats were free, they did not readily yield to the unfair proposal. Their protest against the measure was given by subsequently taking a position near about where they usually occupied. But at length an expressed desire rose to an imperious order, and the pressure was so great, that they considered it useless to contend any longer against the odds that opposed them. The stern command was followed by a forcible act resorted to by one of the officials; and to the lasting shame of those who sanctioned the measure, it was enforced at a time when the assembly were invoking the blessings of the common Father of all, who "IS NO RESPECTER OF PERSONS, AND WILLETH ALL MEN TO BE SAVED AND TO COME TO THE KNOWLEDGE OF THE TRUTH."

This shameful transaction took place on Sunday morning. To use the words of a venerated man—"Meeting had begun, and they were nearly done singing, and just as we took our seats, the Elder said,—LET US PRAY. We had not been long on our knees before I heard considerable scuffling and low talking. I raised my head up and saw one of the trustees having hold of Rev. Absalom Jones, pulling him up off his knees, and saying, "you must get up—you must not kneel here." Mr. Jones replied, "wait until prayer is over." Mr. H. M—— said, "no, you must get up now, or I will call for aid and force you away." Mr. Jones said, "wait until prayer is over, and I will get up and trouble you no more."*

This assurance of Mr. Jones was made good. They all walked out in a body together, and before the close of that eventful Lord's day, the solemn and deliberate purpose, the noble determination, was formed to worship the Lord henceforth under their "own vine and fig tree," without molestation from any. That these humble men, just emerged from the house of bondage, should be able to rise above those servile feelings which all their antecedents were calculated to cherish, and to assume, as they did, an attitude becoming men conscious of invaded rights, is not to be greatly wondered at, when the history of those times is considered. This was the age of a general and searching inquiry into the equity of old and established customs. A moral earthquake had awakened the slumber of ages. The spirit-stirring notes that pealed out from Independence Hall, proclaiming "LIBERTY THROUGHOUT THE LAND TO ALL THE INHABITANTS THEREOF," and causing the most humble to lift up his head with higher hopes and nobler aspirations, were yet echoing through every nook and corner of the land. The revolutionary

---

* Life of Rev. Richard Allen, written by himself, 1833, page 13.

struggle, in which was involved the great principles of human rights, was still fresh in the minds of all from the least unto the greatest. The magnanimous spirit that then prevailed to a very great extent throughout the country, is very beautifully expressed by the Legislature of Pennsylvania in its Act for the gradual abolition of slavery, passed in 1780,—"It is not for us to enquire why, in the creation of mankind, the inhabitants of the several parts of the earth were distinguished by a difference in feature or complexion. It is sufficient to know, that all are the work of an Almighty hand. We esteem it a peculiar blessing granted to us, that we are enabled this day to add one more step to universal civilization, by removing, as much as possible, the sorrows of those, who have lived in undeserved bondage, and from which, by the assumed authority of the kings of Great Britain, no effectual, legal relief could be obtained. Weaned, by a long course of experience, from those narrow prejudices and partialities we had imbibed, we find our hearts enlarged with kindness and benevolence towards men of all conditions and nations; and we conceive ourselves at this particular period extraordinarily called upon, by the blessings which we have received, to manifest the sincerity of our profession, and to give a substantial proof of our gratitude."

Those obscure but worthy men, who, animated with some of the spirit of those days, resolved to introduce a new order of things among themselves, had one great difficulty to surmount, before they could proceed a step towards the accomplishment of the object desired. The great question for solution in the first place, was, how to effect a union among themselves. Unaccustomed to organizations of any kind, few in number, without pecuniary means, the most favored among them without the advantages of a liberal education; to have immediately proposed, under these circumstances, the establishing of a church, would have been considered impracticable and visionary. But a successful plan of union at length presented itself, which was to form an organization having the two-fold objects of a beneficial and moral reform society. It was styled, "The Free African Society," and was founded the 12th of April, in the year of our Lord 1787.

PREAMBLE OF THE FREE AFRICAN SOCIETY

The following is a copy of the Preamble and Articles of the Association, with the names of the First Signers.

"*Philadelphia.*"

"[12th, 4th mo., 1778.]—WHEREAS, Absalom Jones and Richard Allen, two men of the African race, who, for their religious life and conversation have obtained a good report among men, these persons, from a love to the people of their complexion whom they beheld with sorrow, because of their irreligious and uncivilized state, often communed together upon this painful and important subject in order to form some kind of religious society, but there being too few to be found under the like concern, and those who were, differed in their religious sentiments; with these circumstances they labored for some time, till it was proposed, after a serious communication of sentiments, that a society should be formed, without regard to religious tenets, provided, the persons lived an orderly and sober life, in order to support one another in sickness, and for the benefit of their widows and fatherless children."

ARTICLES.

"[17th, 5th mo., 1787.]—We, the free Africans and their descendants, of the City of Philadelphia, in the State of Pennsylvania, or elsewhere, do unanimously agree, for the benefit of each other, to advance one shilling in silver Pennsylvania currency a month; and after one year's subscription from the date hereof, then to hand forth to the needy of this Society, if any should require, the sum of three shillings and nine pence per week of the said money: provided, this necessity is not brought on them by their own imprudence.

And it is further agreed, that no drunkard nor disorderly person be admitted as a member, and if any should prove disorderly after having been received, the said disorderly person shall be disjointed from us if there is not an amendment, by being informed by two of the members, without having any of his subscription money returned.

And if any should neglect paying his monthly subscription for three months, and after having been informed of the same by two of the members, and no sufficient reason appearing for such neglect, if he do not pay the whole the next ensuing meeting, he shall be disjointed from us, by being informed by two of the members as an offender, without having any of his subscription money returned.

Also, if any person neglect meeting every month, for every omission he shall pay three pence, except in case of sickness or any other complaint that should require the assistance of the Society, then, and in such a case, he shall be exempt from the fines and subscription during the said sickness.

Also, we apprehend it to be just and reasonable, that the surviving widow of a deceased member should enjoy the benefit of this Society so long as she remains his widow, complying with the rules thereof, excepting the subscriptions.

And we apprehend it to be necessary, that the children of our deceased members be under the care of the Society, so far as to pay for the education of their children, if they cannot attend the free school; also to put them out apprentices to suitable trades or places, if required.

Also, that no member shall convene the Society together; but, it shall be the sole business of the committee, and that only on special occasions, and to dispose of the money in hand to the best advantage for the use of the Society, after they are granted the liberty at a monthly meeting, and to transact all other business whatsoever, except that of Clerk and Treasurer.

And we unanimously agree to choose Joseph Clarke to be our Clerk and Treasurer; and whenever another should succeed him, it is always understood, that one of the people called Quakers, belonging to one of the three monthly meetings in Philadelphia, is to be chosen to act as Clerk and Treasurer of this useful Institution.

The following persons met, viz., Absalom Jones, Richard Allen, Samuel Baston, Joseph Johnson, Cato Freeman, Cæsar Cranchell, and James Potter, also William White, whose early assistance and useful remarks we found truly profitable. This evening the articles were read, and after some beneficial remarks were made, they were agreed unto."

REMARKS.

This Society, as appears from the minutes, met at the house of Richard Allen, monthly, up to May, 1788. His room at this period being too small for the accommodation of the increased number of members, a more commodious room was rented in the house of Sarah Dougherdy. Here the Society continued its regular meetings up to Dec. 28th, 1788. From this time up to 1791, the monthly meetings were held in "Friends' Free African School House."* At this period, a proposal was made by the Standing Committee of the Society, to establish a religious meeting. This proposition was generally approved of by the members, and the Committee, accordingly, was instructed to procure a room for the purpose. They succeeded in obtaining one of Joseph Sharpless. In this room they met for the first time together for religious worship, January 1st, 1791, at 3 o'clock, P. M.

It will not be uninteresting to observe how gradually they advanced, step by step, to the accomplishment of their ultimate design—the formation of "the African Church."

A very important movement in that direction, was the appointing of a committee, whose business, besides that of calling special meetings, and "disposing of the money in hand to the best advantage," was to inspect the conduct of the members in the interim, and to report the same at one of the

---

* Situated then in Willing's alley, removed since to Raspberry street.

monthly meetings of the Society. The following minute is a record of the first proceedings of said Committee.

"The 17th, 7th mo., 1787.—At a monthly meeting of free Africans, Cæsar Thomas, William White, and Cæsar Cranchell, were appointed to have the oversight of the members this month."

No report appears from this Committee for five successive months, at the expiration of which time it was enlarged, as the following minute shows.

"15th, 12th mo., 1787.—At a monthly meeting of free Africans, held at Philadelphia, Mark Stevenson, Cæsar Thomas, William White, Moses Johnson, Absalom Jones, and Richard Allen, are appointed to visit the members, and give such advice as may appear necessary."

The Report of this Committee appears among the minutes of the subsequent monthly meeting. It reads as follows:

"15th, 1st mo., 1788.

DEAR FRIENDS AND BRETHREN:—

Your Committee are thankful that we are favored with another opportunity of assembling together after this manner, and are pleased with the prospect of an increase in number, as there are daily applications to join the institution. It is the ardent desire of your Committee also, that as we increase in numbers, we may increase in grace and knowledge and every Christian virtue. Although we have not been as diligent in visiting the members this last month as we have formerly, yet, it is not for want of good will: indeed, it hath been of great concern to us that we have not had it in our power, but are in hope, that this duty will be better attended to for the future. We are desirous of laying before you the necessity of handing forth to the sick for another twelve months; our stock is small considering the number of members that are to draw from it. Our stock at present, is but twelve pounds, and if a few sick members should now be supported from it, it would not last us six months. We would have you seriously to think of it, and we doubt not but you will agree to the same.

ABSALOM JONES,
Clerk of the Committee."

To the above report the following resolution is appended, "which was read and approved."

"That no man shall live with any woman as man and wife without she is lawfully his wife, and his certificate must be delivered to the clerk to be put on record."

The first case appearing on the record of disciplinary action against one of the members for immoral conduct, is thus presented by the Committee:

"*Whereas,* Samuel S., one of the members of the Free African Society, held in Philadelphia, for the benefit of the sick, has so shamefully deviated from our known rules, hath often unnecessarily left his tender wife and child, and kept company with a common woman, sometimes quarreling, fighting and swearing, for which he hath been long and tenderly treated with, but he not forsaking his shameful practices, we therefore disown the said Samuel S. from being a member of our Society, till he condemns the same in life and conversation, which is our desire for him.

Signed this 20th of the 9th mo., 1788, on behalf of this Society, by the Committee, viz.:

ABSALOM JONES,
RICHARD ALLEN,
WILLIAM WHITE,
MARK STEVENSON,
WILLIAM GRAY,
CÆSAR CRANCHER,
CÆSAR THOMAS."

The above was read and approved, and the Committtee requested to furnish the said S. S. with a copy.

From all that appears from the minutes, no devotional exercises had hitherto been used at the opening of the meetings of the Society. The first recommendation of any thing of the kind was made by the Committee on the 15th 11th mo., 1788. They having been previously appointed by the Society, reported the following:

"The Committee appointed in the 9th month report, that having taken into their serious consideration, the manner in which this Institution comes together, they have agreed to propose that each member should take his seat at 7 o'clock, and then all be silent till fifteen minutes, after which time the meeting should proceed to business. The meeting, after some time in considering the proposal, unites with and recommends it to all our members."

Considering the previous predilections of a large number of the members composing this Society in favor of an unconstrained outburst of the feelings in religious worship, it is not to be wondered at, that "SOME TIME WAS SPENT IN CONSIDERING THE PROPOSAL;" the only matter of surprise is, that it was adopted at all. That the first meeting held after the adoption of the proposal, was marked with solemn silence during the fifteen minutes agreed upon, is very questionable indeed.

The minutes of this meeting, which agreed upon the form of silent devotion before proceeding to business, show, that the following named persons were present, and severally paid the sum affixed to their names.

"R. Allen, 1; R. Boice, 1; C. Coffee, 1; J. Caton, 3.9; W. Gardiner, 3.9; W. Gray, 1; C. Freeman, 1; A. Jones, 1; J. London, 1; M. Jackson, 1; F. Lewis, 2; M. Read, 1; P. Sharpless, 1; C. Thomas, 1; W. White, 1; Jas. Williams, 6; W. Wilcher, 1; C. Worthington, 1; H. Stewart, 1.—Amount, 31.7½."

It is worthy of notice, that at no succeeding monthly meeting of the Society, does the name of R. Allen appear as an active member among them.

The first record of his name after the meeting last mentioned, is made six months afterwards. It is contained in a report of the Committee to the Society, "held in Philadelphia, at Friends' Free African School House, the 16th of the 5th mo., 1789." The following is a copy of said report:

"The Committee brought in a report concerning Richard Allen* so abruptly leaving the Society, and rashly calling, or convening the members together, contrary to the rules of the Society, but as some tenderness appeared towards him, it was concluded to pay him another visit in brotherly love, and report their sense thereof at the next meeting." Appended to this, is the following record. "Having had the satisfactory company of some Friends, and the business gone through with love and condescension, it is agreed to adjourn to the usual time next month."

"At a monthly meeting of the Free African Society for the benefit of the sick, held in Philadelphia, at Friends' Free African School House, the 20th of the 6th month, 1789, the Committee brought in

* The name of Richard Allen is justly held in high veneration by his people. He evidently saw that the current of religious sentiment in this Society, was not flowing in the direction he desired; hence, he separated, and was eminently successful, finally, in establishing the African Methodist Episcopal Church. He was their first Bishop. The opinion, widely-spread among his people, that he was ordained by the late Bishop White, is erroneous. His Episcopacy stands with Methodism among the whites, upon the same basis. The tie of warm friendship between Absalom Jones and Richard Allen, continued unbroken until they were separated by death.

a testification against Richard Allen, which, being twice deliberately read, was approved, and is as follows, viz.:

We, the Society of Free Africans in the City of Philadelphia, having, according to discipline established among us, long treated with Richard Allen, one of our members, for attempting to sow division among us, and endeavoring to convince him of his error in so doing, and of the breach of good order which he has thereby committed, but finding him refractory, and declaring that he no longer considers himself a member of our Society, do find it our duty to declare that he has disunited himself from membership with us by refusing to submit himself to the rules of the Society, and to attend our meeting, and he is accordingly disunited until he shall come to a sense of his conduct, and request to be admitted a member according to our discipline. Signed by the Committee, viz.:

WM. WHITE,
CÆSAR WORTHINGTON,
CÆSAR THOMAS,
HENRY STEWART,
PETER MILLER,
NATHAN GRAY,
MARK STEVENSON."

The Committee made a proposal to choose Absalom Jones and Moses Johnson, overseers, which is as follows: "Philadelphia, 27th of 5th mo., 1789.—We, the Committee, unanimously agree, after calmly and deliberately weighing the state of the Society, that as much business is likely to arise among us, therefore, for the health of the Society, and the better preservation of her members, do propose Absalom Jones and Moses Johnson, overseers; and the business of the said overseers is to inspect into the necessities of the poor, and to admonish the disorderly; also to inform the Committee of those who are obstinate. And it is proposed, that the Committee shall choose the overseers, and lay the same before the monthly meeting for their approbation; and it is always to be understood, that the overseers are to be sober and exemplary members, and men of good report. No limited time is set for the overseers to remain in that station."

"At a monthly meeting of the Free African Society held in Philadelphia, at Friends' Free African School-house, the 17th, 10th mo., 1789. an epistle was read from the Union Society of Africans in Newport, and another from Boston, together with a certificate of Henry Stewart, all of which are as follows:

DEAR FRIENDS AND BRETHREN:—

We the members of the Union Society, being forty in number, in the town of Newport, consisting of free Africans, have lately had the pleasure of being informed of the formation of your Society in Philadelphia, for the good purposes therein mentioned, by one of your members, Mr. Henry Stewart, who comes recommended by your committee. We taking into consideration the calamitous state into which we are brought by the righteous hand of God, being strangers and outcasts in a strange land, attended with many disadvantages and evils which are likely to continue on us and our children, while we and they live in this country, and yet more wretched state of thousands of our brethren who are in the most abject state of slavery in the West Indies and in the American States, many of whom are treated in the most inhuman and cruel manner, and are sunk down in ignorance, stupidity and vice. And considering the unhappy state and circumstances of our brethren, the nations in Africa from whom we sprung being in heathenish darkness and barbarity, and that it hath pleased God of late to raise up many to compassionate and befriend the Africans, not only in promoting their freedom and using means for their instruction, but by proposing and endeavoring to effect their return to their own country, and their settlement there, where they may be more happy than they can be here, and promote the best good of our brethren in that country. We, taking all this into view, think there is a special and loud call to us, and all the blacks in America, to seek God by extraordinary fasting and prayer, and do therefore request all who are disposed, to join in fasting and prayer to Almighty God, by meeting together for that purpose, privately or in public, as shall be most convenient, on the first Tuesday in July, and on the first day of every year, humbly to confess the sins of our fathers, and our own sins, and to acknowledge the righteousness of God in bringing all these evils on us and on our children and brethren; and earnestly to cry to God for the pardon of our sins, and that he would of his great mercy deliver us and our brethren, and the nations in Africa, from the sins and miseries in which we and they are now involved, and pour down his Holy Spirit upon us, and cause us and them to become a wise, virtuous, and Christian people. And that he would in his wise and good Providence prosper the way for our returning to Africa, and direct, assist, and prosper all our friends who are engaged in this cause, that he would give us favor in the eyes of our brethren in Africa, and raise up friends and benefactors in this land who shall be willing and able to promote this important affair, and that God would in his great mercy succeed them and us in all endeavors for this end; that the Father of mercies would bless all the nations who enjoy the gospel, and cause them to conduct themselves agreeable to it, by doing to all men as they would others should do unto them, that the light of it may spread over all the world.

ANTHONY TAYLOR, *President*,
KINGSTON PEASE, *Vice*,
PRINCE AMY,
ZINGO STEVENS,
SALMAR NUBIA,
THOMAS FERGUSON.

These black gentlemen are at present Freeholders and members of the Union Society, chosen at our annual meeting the 13th Aug., 1789, in Newport, Rhode Island.

JAMES DYRE,
BACCUS OVERING,
WILLIAM HENSHAW,
BACCUS COGGESHALL,
BESS BROWNING,
REBECCA FOLGER,

Freeholders, and not belonging to the Union Society, Newport, Sep. 1st, 1789.

P. S.—

GENTLEMEN:

The above and foregoing persons are all the Freeholders of blacks belonging to the town of Newport. Mr. Henry Stewart having paid us a visit, on his way for Boston, with your certificate, it appears to us that he is well deserving.

REPLY TO THE FOREGOING BY THE COMMITTEE.

RESPECTED FRIENDS:

We read your epistle dated the 1st of the 9th mo., (called September,) 1789, which claimed our serious attention, and we are apprehensive that a lively and religious correspondence would be conducive to our religious improvement. With regard to the emigration to Africa you mention, we have at present but little to communicate on that head, apprehending every pious man is a good citizen of the whole world. Therefore, let us, as with the heart of one man, continue daily in fasting and prayer,—fasting from sin and iniquity and the corrupt conversation of the world, that the Lord thereby may be pleased to break every yoke, and let the oppressed go free. And it is a certain prophecy that swords shall be beat into ploughshares, and spears into pruning hooks, that nation shall not lift up sword against nation, neither shall they learn war any more. A happy day that will prove to us of the African race, and mankind in general; then captivity shall cease, and buying and selling mankind have an end; we have a well grounded hope that the knowledge of the Lord will cover the earth, as the waters cover the sea. Now we have to behold with humble admiration, that this prophecy is fulfilling daily for us, (O, that we may be sensible of so great a favor,) seeing the Lord is raising up many to promote this peaceable kingdom with no other weapons than that of giving glory to God, and breathing peace and good will towards men, persons who are sacrificing their own time, ease and property for us, the stranger and the fatherless, in this wilderness, these persons declare in the expressive language of conduct, that they are followers of Him who taught his disciples to do unto all men as we would they should do unto us. Howbeit, if any apprehend a divine injunction is laid upon them to undertake such a long and perilous journey in order to promote piety and virtue, that such may meet with encouragement is the sincere desire of a remnant, and that the arm of divine protection may continually hover over them."

CERTIFICATE TO H. STEWART.

NEWPORT, *Aug.* 22*nd*, 1789.

These are to certify, that the bearer, Mr. Henry Stewart, one of the members of the Freeholders, African Society, established in the City of Philadelphia for the benefit of the sick of said society, and other commendable purposes, has been with us as a traveler, and has behaved himself as a truly worthy member, and as such we recommend him to all our friends, more particularly to the African Company now in the town of Boston.

ANTHONY TAYLOR, *President*,
KINGSTON PEASE, *Vice*,
Of the Union Society in Newport.

BOSTON LETTER.

BOSTON, *Sep.* 16*th*, 1789.

DEAR BRETHREN OF THE AFRICAN SOCIETY:

These lines come to acquaint you, that we have your recommended brother, Mr. Henry Stewart, and am happy to hear that you have such a society built on so laudable a foundation. May God prosper you in this and all your undertakings for the good of your African brethren. I hope you will go on and prosper. I shall be always happy in hearing of your welfare. We here, are not idle, but are doing what we can to promote the interest and good of our dear brethren that stand in so much need at such a time as this. We shall be glad therefore, to hear of your proceedings, by letters of correspondence with us.

Your brother Stewart will inform you by word of mouth of some proposals we made to him, which I do not care to write at this time. No more at present, but remain,

Your loving brother,
Farewell,
PRINCE HALL.*

REPLY.

"DEAR BRETHREN,—

We read your epistle by the hand of Henry Stewart, one of our members, who visited you. It afforded us matter of satisfaction, to find that you are united with us in laboring in the same vineyard, we seriously hope to the honor of God and the benefit of mankind.

May you steadily continue in this labor, for the harvest is truly great, but the sincere and disinterested laborers are few. Notwithstanding, let none be discouraged, however low their station among men may be,—for we find in holy writ, that the race is not to the swift, nor the battle to the strong; but that one who has on the shield of faith, shall chase a thousand, and two put ten thousand to flight. Here is encouragement for us of the African race. The scriptures declare, that, God is no respecter of persons. We beseech you, therefore, in much brotherly love, to lay aside all superfluity of naughtiness, especially gaming and feast-

* Distinguished as the first colored Grand Master Mason in the United States.

ing; a shameful practice, that we as a people are particularly guilty of. While we are feasting and dancing, many of our complexion are starving under cruel bondage; and it is this practice of ours that enables our enemies to declare that we are not fit for freedom,—and at the same time, this imprudent conduct stops the mouths of our real friends, who would ardently plead our cause. Let us therefore, dear brethren, learn to be wise by fearing the Lord, and shew that we have a good understanding by forsaking our foolish practices.

Now unto Him who is able to keep us from falling, and present us faultless before the presence of his glory with exceeding joy, to the only wise God our Saviour be glory and majesty, dominion and power, both now and ever. Amen.

Read and approved at our monthly meeting, and signed by the committee and clerk, on behalf of the same.

BALANCE IN TREASURER'S HANDS.

At a monthly meeting of the Free African Society, held in Philadelphia, for the benefit of the sick, at Friends' Free School-house, the 15th of the 1st mo., 1790.

The Treasurer producing the money in his possession, and it being at this time examined, there appeared a balance in favor of the Society of forty-two pounds, nine shilling, and one penny, and as divers members think a propriety would attend a deposite of this balance in the Bank of North

America, he is desired to lodge it there on behalf of the Society as soon as convenient, and report his performance of the business at next meeting."

"At a monthly meeting of the Free African Society, 20th of 2nd mo., 1790, our worthy friend and kind assistant Joseph Clark, whose remarkable attention to the welfare of this institution demands our most grateful acknowledgments, requesting a release from the clerkship of this Society, the meeting considering the request as reasonable, agreed to it, and said Joseph Clark and our committee having united in mentioning the name of George Williams as a proper person to be clerk, and a concurring sentiment prevailing with divers members, the society after deliberate and weighty consideration, concluded to request him to act in that capacity, and said George Williams being now present, and submitting to the wishes of the Society, it is expected he will assist us in that way. Notwithstanding, this meeting has agreed to release our friend Joseph Clark from the clerkship, yet, he being willing to concur with our wishes in remaining as treasurer to the institution, he is continued in that station.

The treasurer reports his having lodged the Society's money at the Bank of N. America, which has opened an account with him as treasurer to this institution."

"At a monthly meeting of the Free African Society, 20th of 3rd mo., 1790.

The stranger's burial ground in this City,

4

usually called the Potter's Field, being offered to be let by the corporation of the City, our overseers and committee have apprehended that a great propriety would attend this Society's having the care of said ground, and therefore called a special meeting the 13th inst., when, after the subject was attentively considered, a petition to the Mayor, Aldermen, and Common Councilmen was agreed to, and is as follows:

To the worshipful, the Mayor, Aldermen and Common Councilmen, of the City of Philadelphia, in Common Council.

The petition of the Free African Society for the benefit of the sick, in the City of Philadelphia,

RESPECTFULLY SHEWETH:

That the burial-ground called the Potter's field, being in part appropriated for the burial of black persons, and chiefly made use of for that purpose, and your petitioners being informed that the Common Council are about to let the same, are desirous to have the said burial-ground under the care of the said Society, and are willing to pay the same rent that hath been offered by any other person, and a year's advance as soon as the said ground is enclosed, and they are put in possession thereof.

They therefore pray that the said ground may be rented to them for one or more years, on the terms they propose, and under such regulations as the Common Council shall think proper to make.

And your petitioners shall pray.

Signed on behalf of the same, by

MOSES JOHNSON,
ABSALOM JONES, } *Overseers.*

CYRUS BUSTILL,
WILLIAM WHITE,
HENRY STEWART,
TOD FINCH,
ABRAHAM INGLIS,
JAMES CATON. } *Committee.*

ENDORSEMENT ON THE BACK OF THE PETITION.

We, the subscribers, having for some time past been acquainted with several of the members of the 'FREE AFRICAN SOCIETY, ESTABLISHED IN THE CITY OF PHILADELPHIA, FOR THE BENEFIT OF SUCH AMONG THEM WHO MAY BECOME INFIRM,' do certify, that we have informed ourselves of the rules and order established by the said Society, and approve of their Institution, and can therefore recommend the members thereof, as well their humane design, to the notice and attention of their fellow citizens, they being worthy of a degree of confidence and encouragement.

(Signed) GEO. WILLIAMS, BENJ. RUSH,
WM. ASHBY, NICHOLAS WALN,
JOSEPH CLARK, WILLIAM WHITE,
SAM'L MAGAW, CHARLES WILLIAMS,
TENCH COXE, JOSEPH JAMES,
WILLIAM SAVERY."

REPORT CONCERNING MARRIAGE.

"Our Committee, at a meeting of them, the 15th of the present month, having taken into view a concern which has attended the minds of divers members for several years, and at the time of their last meeting weightily renewed, that a way might be opened for such of our members and others as were inclined to accomplish their intentions of marriage at one of our meetings in a sober and reputable way, taking care that parents and others concerned be consulted and consent obtained, and everything else connected with such a proceeding made as conformable to propriety as might be; the Society now entered into a serious and deliberate consideration of the subject, and being united in sentiment with the Committee, are concerned that every necessary caution may be taken in order to establish a regular mode of procedure with respect to such marriages as may be accomplished before us, as well as a proper form of the necessary certificate and book of records thereof.

Cyrus Bustill, Absalom Jones, William White, Cæsar Cranchell, Henry Steward, Moses Johnson, and Cato Freeman, are appointed to take these matters into their special consideration, and report to the next meeting what may appear to them necessary."

"At a monthly meeting of the Free African Society, the 17th day of 4th mo., 1790.

Cyrus Bustill and others, appointed a committee

for the consideration of regulations with respect to the mode of marriage as proposed by our former committee, brought in the following report:

Your committee, after several sittings, and weightily considering the subject referred to them, have freedom to offer for your deliberation the following mode of procedure proposed to be adopted and continued in, until experience shall point out amendments therein.

1st. When any persons are desirous of marrying amongst us, the man is to inform one of the committee or overseers of such intentions; it shall then be the business of the committee and overseers to inquire whether the parents and friends of the parties are consenting, and if no objection appears, they may give information to the monthly meeting, and there produce such consent as they may have obtained.

2nd. After the society are informed of any intended marriage, the committee shall make enquiry what time will be most suitable to the parties concerned, and call a meeting for the purpose, informing the members generally thereof, who are enjoined to attend and support a solemnity suited to the occasion. Men and women of sober deportment to be invited by the committee to come and sit with us in the meeting.

3rd. The form of the certificate to be nearly as the following:

"*Whereas*, A. B., son of A. B., of the City of P., and State of P., and S. T., daughter of S. T., of same City and State, having declared their intentions of marriage with each other before several members of the 'African Society for the Benefit of the Sick,' and also obtained the consent of parents and relations concerned, their said proposals were allowed of by the society.

Now these are to certify all whom it may concern, that for the full accomplishing their said intentions this day of the month, they the said A. B. and S. T., appeared before several members of the above said Society, at their meeting-house in Philadelphia, and the said A. B. taking the said S. T. by the hand, did in a solemn manner openly declare that he took the said S. T. to be his wife, promising through divine assistance to be unto her a loving and faithful husband until death should separate them,—and then and there in the same assembly the said S. T. did in like manner openly declare that she took the said A. B. to be her husband, promising through divine assistance to be unto him a loving and faithful wife until death should separate them.

Moreover, they the said A. B. and S. T., (she according to the custom of marriage assuming the name of her husband,) as a further confirmation thereof did then and there to these presents set their hands.

A. B.
S. T.

And we whose names are hereunto also subscribed being present at the solemnization of said marriage and subscription, have as witnesses thereunto set our hands, the day and year above written.

4th. A book for the record of certificates to be procured, and our clerk desired to enter such certificates."

"The following persons, members of the 'Society for the gradual abolition of Slavery,' having attended this meeting, viz., Thomas Harrison, Amos Gregg, Nathan Boys, John Todd, and John Evans, who informing us of the plan of their society for the improving the condition of the free blacks, and that the abolition society, in order to promote our happiness, had gone into the appointment of the following committees. 1st. A committee of inspection. 2nd. A committee of guardians. 3rd. A committee of education, and 4th. A committee of employ: and in order to facilitate an enquiry into the condition of the free blacks, it was proposed that a committee be appointed by this Society to accompany them in the business.

Wm. Wiltshire, Cyrus Bustill, Cæsar Cranshell, Moses Johnson, Absalom Jones, Abraham Inglis, William White, and Ceasar Thomas, are desired to give attention to this business and report thereon."

"At a monthly meeting of the Free African Society, held the 15th of 5th mo., 1790.

The committee named last month to assist the deputation from the Society for the gradual abolition of 'Slavery,' in endeavoring to ascertain the number of free blacks in this city, having paid a close attention to their appointment, and procured lists of families, &c., in the districts, of the city and liberties, they furnished the deputation* with them, and believing the service sufficiently completed, it is now concluded to release them."

The next thing worthy of special notice is the proposal of the committee for a *religious meeting*, offered for the consideration of the Society, the 18th of Sep., 1790. It is as follows:

"The committee having been thoughtful respecting a religious meeting being established by this Society, propose, that, as the Society are bound in gratitude to the Divine Being by many obligations, a religious meeting for the performance of divine worship and grateful acknowledgement, be opened on the third 1st day in every month, at 3 o'clock in the afternoon, at such place as may be procured; and that no approved minister be prohibited from attending, or speaking at it.

Although this proposal met with general approbation, yet the measure being important, the subject is agreed to remain under consideration till next meeting."

---

* The committee of inspection reported "about 250 families in the City, Northern Liberties and Southwark, making nearly 1,000 persons of both sexes, almost 400 of whom were minors." For this important item, we are indebted to the kindness of Mr. Truman, Secretary of the old Abolition Society.

At a monthly meeting of the Free African Society, held the 16th day of the 10th mo., 1790, the overseers report that a visit has been paid to the members generally, and that no breach of good order was observed. This account is satisfactory to the meeting, and they are desired to continue their care in visiting and strengthening the members in a virtuous life. The proposal of holding a religious meeting being again resumed, it is now united with, and is agreed that the committee be requested to procure a suitable place for the purpose, and notify the meeting next month, that our members may be informed and desired to attend."

"20th of 11th mo. Wm. White, on behalf of the committee, informs us that a room for holding a religious meeting is not yet procured; this subject is continued under their care."

"18th of 12th mo., 1790. It appears that the committee have been further attentive to procuring a room for holding a religious meeting, in which however, they have not as yet succeeded, although there is a probability that by next month they will receive an answer respecting one in particular, for which they have applied.

"They are requested to attend further to the business."

"15th of 1st mo., 1791. The committee now report that they have not yet been able to procure a room in which a religious meeting may be constantly held, although they have had permission to hold a meeting to-morrow afternoon, in a room of

Joseph Sharpless, which they have concluded to open at 3 o'clock. Their proceedings are agreeable to the meeting, and they are expected to continue attentive to procuring a permanent place of meeting."

"19th of 2nd mo., 1791. By a minute of the committee, it appears that a religious meeting was held at the time mentioned last month, and was attended with much satisfaction; they likewise mention, that although they have not succeeded in obtaining a place to meet in, which promises a long continuance, yet, there is a great probability that the present place may be made use of for a considerable time hence. It is now agreed that the said meeting be held on the first day of the week, immediately following the meeting of this Society, until otherwise directed."

"19th of 3rd mo. Absalom Jones informed the meeting that another satisfactory religious meeting had been held. This information affords the members present particular pleasure. The overseers report that in a late visit to the members in their families, generally, every thing appeared to be conducted in a reputable manner."

"16th 4th mo., 1791. A religious meeting has been held in course since last month, and was satisfactory. The overseers since last month, have been with divers members in their families; nothing new or unusual occurred."

"21st 5th mo., 1791. Two religious meetings are reported to have been held since last month. The overseers have seen divers members in their families since last month, to satisfaction, and expect to visit all, previous to next meeting."

"17th 2nd mo., 1792. It appears from the title deed, that the lots on which St. Thomas' Church edifice now stands, were purchased "by Wm. Gray, Absalom Jones, Wm. White, Wm. Wiltshire, Wm. Gardiner and Henry Stewart, of Joseph B. McKean and Hannah his wife," on the day and date above written, "for the sum of four hundred and fifty pounds, lawful money of the State of Pennsylvania, each lot containing in breadth, north and south, twenty-six feet, and in length and depth, east and west, one hundred and ninety-eight feet and six inches." The bona fide title to these lots was vested in the above-named individuals; but, that they acted for, and were regarded by the congregation as their trustees only, will hereafter be seen."

"18th 2nd mo., 1792. The committee delivered the following report: that no member should interrupt another in speaking, but, to speak mildly, one at a time, and that the overseers should sit at the desk with the clerk, and command order if necessary; also, a further report in regard to examining the accounts, which was satisfactory, and a clear report in regard to the cash book belonging to the treasurer; likewise the bank book, in hands, which is plain and satisfactory."

"28th 2nd mo., 1792. These are to certify, that on the aforegoing day and date, Wm. White and Absalom Jones called on Joseph Sharpless, and entered into an agreement with him for his school-house, for the use of the African Church, at the rate of five pounds per year, from the first of January, 1792; and to make him up eight dollars for the first year we had the school-house for that purpose, and to pay the usher three dollars for the trouble he has had for the first year."

"23rd 3rd mo. 1792. The representatives of the African Church met together, and after communication of sentiments, agreed to take the cash in hand, and get some subscription papers drawn up, and to collect as fast as possible."

"5th mo. 16th, 1792. At a special meeting of the Free African Society, held at the school-house on Friends' Alms-house lot, a conference was had respecting the appropriation of one hundred dollars out of the monthly meeting stock belonging to the said Free African Society, towards the purchase of a lot for the use of the Society, it was agreed that the same be applied accordingly; for although it appears by the minutes that the stock was intended for the relief of the poor among them, yet, under all the circumstances, it was thought advisable for the sake of peace and harmony, to agree to the said appropriation.

NICHOLAS WALN,
WILLIAM ROGERS,
MIERS FISHER,
—— FITZGERALD.

"NOTE. The persons whose names are here inserted, were present at said meeting."

"19th 5th mo., 1792. At a monthly meeting of the Free African Society, held in Philadelphia, for the benefit of the sick, the committee appointed in a difficult case, brought in a report, which being read, signifying that they had agreed that one hundred dollars should be handed out of the treasury for the use of the African Church, was approved by the meeting, and Absalom Jones was appointed to call on the treasurer for the same."

"21st 7th mo., 1792. At a monthly meeting of the Free African Society, one of the overseers reported the following, which was adopted.

Whereas, some difference of opinion has subsisted between some of the members respecting the powers of this Society to appropriate a sum of money towards purchasing a lot for the purpose of erecting a place of worship for the use of this Society, which difference having arisen from the omission of entering the minute of the 28th of the 7th month, 1791; and as the subject has obtained the deliberate consideration of this Society for some meetings past, as well as several well wishers to our Society, it is now agreed that the said minute of the 28th of the 7th month, 1791, be annexed to the minutes in its proper place, and that our future transactions be conducted conformable thereto. The minute being as follows:

At a special meeting of the Free African Society, convened by direction of the standing committee, a plan of church government, and articles of faith and practice, suited to the establishment of a religious society being read, the Society concluded to unite therewith, and also with an address to the friends of liberty and religion in Philadelphia, and to appoint Absalom Jones to prepare said address."

At this place we turn over a new leaf. The sayings and doings of the old "Free African Society," as such, now come to a close, and that Association might be left to stand by itself as a solitary but pleasing reminiscence of the past, were it not so intimately connected with what still remains in active operation, and into which it so beautifully merges. Watching the progressive movements of this Society, has been exceedingly gratifying to our feelings. Its noble aim in the first place, was to call out in active operation the humane and tender sympathies of the heart towards the sick and needy. It soon afterward became alive to the importance of the intellectual and moral improvement of the race; and finally, it reorganizes for the purpose of promoting the interests of that divine scheme, which is the only true elevator of mankind—the gospel of Christ. At this incipient stage of St. Thomas' Church, we now enter upon the task of recording its annals.

The officers of this new organization are styled "elders and deacons of the African Church;" and the first business attended to, subsequent to the last meeting held, was to satisfy all such members who preferred to withdraw the money they had invested in the old Society, to having it transferred to the funds of the new enterprise. This, the following minute shows.

"Nov. 3rd, 1792. At a meeting of the Elders and Deacons of the African Church, the members of the Free African Society being convened together, the question was asked the members, separately, whether they design to continue in the Church, or whether they prefer to withdraw the money they placed in the Society.

11th mo., 3rd, 1792. I do hereby certify, that the money I subscribed to the African Society, I freely give to the church.

CYRUS BUSTILL.

his
Ditto, ... JOHN ⋈ MORRIS.
mark.

his
Ditto, ... SAM'L ⋈ BOSTON.
mark.

After the above members had made a deed of gift of the money they had in stock, the following named members claimed what they had invested.

JAMES MINTESS,
MOSES JOHNSON,
WILLIAM BURROWS,
WILLIAM WILTSHIRE,
ISRAEL DE SILVER,
MARK STEPHENSON,
FRANCIS LEWIS,
CÆSAR CRANCHELL,
THOMAS HENDERSON."

"Dec. 12th, 1792. At a meeting of the Elders and Deacons of the African Church, held at the house of James Dexter, members present,—

Wm. White, Absalom Jones, John Emory, Doras Jennings, James Dexter, Alexander Cicero, William Gray, and Cæsar Worthington.

It was on motion,

Resolved, That Absalom Jones and Wm. Gray be appointed to go with Joseph Clark on Friday the 14th inst., to the Bank, and there receive from him his authority for their receiving out of the Bank the balance dueto the African Society."

"Dec. 18th, 1792. At a meeting of the Elders and Deacons, &c., held at the house of John Emory, Absalom Jones reported that he and Wm. Gray, in accordance with the resolution at our last meeting, waited on Joseph Clark, went with him to the Bank, and received the balance due to the African Society.

It was then on motion,

Resolved, That our next meeting be at the house of Cæsar Worthington, at 7 o'clock to-morrow evening, for the purpose of paying the balances due to such members of the African Society as demand the same; and that James Mintess, Israel De Silver, Moses Johnson, Mark Stephenson, William Wiltshire, Francis Wiltshire, Francis Lewis, and William Burris, be notified of said meeting, in order that they may attend and receive their respective claims.

Resolved, That Cæsar Worthington and Cyrus Porter be appointed to notify them of the same."

"Dec. 19th, 1792. At a meeting of the Elders and Deacons, &c., held at the house of Cæsar Worthington,

Present,

Elders.	*Deacons.*
Absalom Jones,	William Gray,
William White,	William Gardiner,
John Emory,	Cyrus Porter,
Doras Jenings,	Cæsar Worthington.
James Dexter,	
Alexander Cicero.	

The business of the evening commenced by paying the balances claimed by the following named persons belonging to the African Society: James Mintess, Israel De Silver, Moses Johnson, Mark Stephenson, Francis Lewis, William Wiltshire, and Peter Sharpless. Peter Sharpless, after giving his receipt of the balance due him, generously returned it for the use of the African Church."

"Jan. 17th, 1793. At a meeting of the Elders and Deacons, &c., held at the house of James Dexter,

Present,

Elders.	*Deacons.*
Absalom Jones,	William Gray,
Wm. White,	Cyrus Porter,
John Emory,	Wm. Gardiner,
Doras Jennings,	Cæsar Worthington.
James Dexter,	
Alexander Cicero.	

Mr. Robins the bricklayer, and Cyrus Bustill, appeared and produced an estimate for the building, as follows:

Bricklayer's estimate for materials, &c.,	£483	1	4
" " workmanship,	215	0	0
	£698	1	4
Carpenter's estimate, including all workmanship and all other expenses incident to the same, ...	£637	6	0
	£1,335	7	4

Resolved, That a committee of three be appointed, namely, Absalom Jones, Wm. Gray and Cæsar Worthington, to consider the above estimates, and set forth the ways and means by which such sums can be raised, in order to meet the expenses to be incurred. The said committee are hereby authorized to call in any person or persons to assist them with their advice."

"Jan. 18th, 1793. At a meeting of the Elders and Deacons, &c., held at the house of Absalom Jones,

Present,

Elders.	*Deacons.*
Absalom Jones,	Wm. Gray,
Wm. White,	Wm. Gardner,
John Emory,	Cyrus Porter,
Doras Jennings,	Cæsar Worthington.
Alex. Cicero.	

Agreeably to the resolution of last meeting, Absalom Jones, William Gray, and Cæsar Worthington, appointed to consider and make a report on the ways and means for raising the sum or sums of money sufficient to defray the expenses to be incurred in building the African Church, brought in their report, which is as follows:—That they have applied to Jno. Nicholson, Esq., who proposes to lend them the sum of two thousand dollars, which sum, the committee states may be laid out in the following manner.

1st. To purchase the bricks, lime, sand and stone.

2nd. To purchase scantling, boards, shingles, nails, &c.

		£	s	d
Bricklayer's estimate for materials, .		£483	1	4
Carpenter's do. do. .		287	6	0
		£770	7	4
Amount furnished by Mr. Nicholson,		750	0	0
Deficient on this account, ...		£20	7	4
Bricklayer's charge for himself, and those he employs, .	£215			
Carpenter's do. do. .	350			
		565	0	0
Deficiency on the whole, ...		£585	7	4

This deficiency it appears to us cannot at present be made up; and without some further plan be adopted in order to obtain it, the attempt to commence the work of building will be vain. As the money to be advanced by Mr. Nicholson is appropriated to the purchasing of the materials, we must by all means provide for the immediate payment of those employed to carry on the work: for which purpose, we propose that an additional sum of *one thousand dollars* be borrowed for the above mentioned purpose. This we judge, with the subscriptions that may be collected, will be sufficient for the present. After we shall have negotiated for the loan of *three thousand dollars,* the deficiency still to be met will be £210 7 4, which sum we must exert ourselves to collect from the gentlemen who have already subscribed, and from such others as are disposed to encourage our undertaking.

Signed, ABSALOM JONES,
WM. GRAY,
CÆSAR WORTHINGTON. } *Committee.*

CYRUS BUSTILL* was called in by the committee for his advice, &c.

Resolved, That the above report of the committee be, and is hereby unanimously agreed to by the members present, and that the said loans be perfected as soon as possible, in order that the work may be forwarded with all reasonable despatch.

---

* Cyrus Bustill was generally respected for his uprightness, and much relied upon by his brethren for his sound judgment. He was the first to relinquish his claim on the old Society in behalf of the church. This noble act appears to good advantage, in view of his religious sentiments, which accorded with those of the Friends. He was the father of David Bustill, widely known in this city as a man of high moral worth, and who clings with tenacity to the religious tenets of his father.

Resolved, That Absalom Jones, William Gray, and Cæsar Worthington, be, and they are hereby appointed a committee to negotiate for the above sum of *three thousand dollars,* so that the work intended may be brought to perfection as soon as possible."

"Feb. 10th, 1793. The trustees of the African Church think it a duty incumbent upon them to make known to the congregation the result of their proceedings in regard to what they have done towards building the church.

1st. They take this mode of informing the congregation at large, that they have borrowed a sum of money for the purpose of erecting the building, for which there is an annual interest to be paid, quarterly, and for which there is no fund, as yet provided.

2nd. They therefore make the following proposals; that (if agreeable to the congregation) a monthly collection be made for the above mentioned purpose of paying said interest.

3rd. That should there be an overplus after paying said interest, the sum shall go towards paying the principal debt, and the other exigencies of the church.

4th. There shall be a fair and regular account kept of all the expenses attending the erecting of the building; likewise of all the moneys received for the support and use of the church.

5th. There shall be a fair statement of the same made out when the building is finished, for the satisfaction and inspection of the congregation, or sooner, if it be found necessary.

6th. They therefore appoint Sunday the 17th inst., to make the first collection, and on every first Sunday in each succeeding month.

The Elders and Deacons also desire, that a decent decorum may be observed at the time of public worship, for which reason they recommend the following rules, viz.:

1st. That at the time of singing, praise, &c., to our Maker, the congregation shall stand or keep seated, as they may find freedom.

2nd. They recommend the congregation to supply themselves with such books as are necessary, so that they may read, sing, and praise the Lord in harmony, with universal heart and voice."

"Feb. 11th. 1793. At a meeting of the Trustees, Elders and Deacons, held at the house of William White, the Committee appointed to report ways and means for erecting the African church, report, that they have negotiated a loan of TWO THOUSAND dollars for said purpose.

Resolved, That James Dexter be appointed to purchase 150 perches of stone, to be delivered on the premises, on as reasonable terms as possible, taking the person's obligation for the punctual delivery of the same in a specified time.

Resolved, That Wm. White be appointed to purchase or procure a lime-house, to be removed on the premises as soon as possible.

Resolved, That Wm. Gray be appointed to purchase the lime.

Resolved, That Absalom Jones, Wm. Gray and Wm. Wiltshire be appointed to treat with the carpenter in regard to the materials.

Resolved, That Absalom Jones and James Dexter do apply to Mr. Cripps, and ascertain upon what terms he will furnish 160,000 bricks, for the purpose of building the church."

"Feb. 26th, 1793. At a meeting of the Trustees, Elders and Deacons of the African church—Wm. White reports that he has attended to the business for which he was appointed at the last meeting, respecting a lime-house, and says, that Col. Francis Johnson has kindly made a present of a lime-house for the use of the church.

James Dexter reports that he has purchased 150 perches of stone, to be delivered on the spot, at 6.9 per perch.

Absalom Jones reports, that he has agreed with Peter Bobb for 150,000 bricks, at 32.6 per thousand, and that Mr. B. says he will make a present to the Church of 3,000 bricks, on condition that we advance him the sum of two hundred dollars when the kiln is burning. He gives satisfactory security for the punctual delivery of the same when required.

Resolved, That Absalom Jones be authorized to perfect the agreement with Mr. Bobb.

Wm. Gray reports, that he has delivered the

draft of the building, and bill of scantling to Messrs. Summers & Worrell, and that they are gone to the Mill to procure the timber."

"March 5th, 1793. At a meeting of the Trustees, Elders and Deacons, held at the house of Wm. White—Cyrus Porter reports, that he has waited on Messrs. Summers & Worrell, and also on Mr. Robins, and that they have agreed to meet the officers of the church on the lot to-morrow morning, at 10 o'clock, to mark out the ground where the foundation is to be digged.

Absalom Jones reports, that he and Wm. Gray had engaged bricks sufficient for the building, at 32.6 per thousand, of Mr. Bobb and Mr. Hansman."

"March 12th, 1793. At a meeting of the Trustees, &c., held at the house of Jno. Emory, Cyrus Porter reports, that agreeable to his appointment to procure poles for the church, he has obtained the number of thirty, at 6 per piece.

James Dexter reports that Magnus Miller, who has the disposal of certain materials, such as sashes, doors, window-shutters, glass, &c., &c., belonging to the Presbyterian meeting-house in Market street, is willing to treat with us and sell the same, for the use of the African church. We therefore appoint Wm. Gray and Cæsar Worthington to treat with Mr. Miller for the said materials, with the assistance of Messrs. Summers & Worrell."

"March 19th, 1793. At a meeting of the Trustees, &c., held at the house of Wm. White, Cyrus

Porter reports that he has purchased twelve scaffold poles, in addition to the thirty he reported at the last meeting, for the use of the church.

The members present taking into consideration the propriety of building the church further back on the lot, resolved to build it where the cellar is now being dug.

Wm. Gray reports that lime is now one-quarter of a dollar per bushel, but expects it will be cheaper when the roads get better, at which time he will, agreeable to his appointment, make the purchase."

"May 21st, 1793. At a meeting of the Elders, &c., held at the house of Wm. White, Absalom Jones reports that he and Wm. Gray have received the additional sum of one thousand dollars from Mr. Nicholson, and placed it in the hands of Mr. Ralston. He also reports that he has paid Mr. Nicholson one quarter's interest.

Any further details of reports, &c., respecting the progress of the work, we conceive to be unnecessary; sufficient have been given to evince the great prudence, energy, zeal, faithfulness and perseverance those humble, but noble, pioneers displayed in entering upon and carrying on to its completion the great and good work they had in hand. It will be a more interesting picture to behold the Building prepared and opened for the first time for public worship, July 17th, 1794.

A

DISCOURSE

Delivered July 17th, 1794, in the

AFRICAN CHURCH

Of the City of Philadelphia,

on the occasion of opening the said Church, and holding public worship in it the first time,

By SAMUEL MAGAW, D.D.,

Rector of St. Paul's.

DIVINE SERVICE,

introduced with select scripture passages, and a special prayer, and then, proceeding in its usual offices, having been performed by

THE REV. JAMES ABERCROMBIE, A. M.,

Second Assistant Minister of Christ Church and St. Peter's.

"Ethiopia shall soon stretch out her hands unto God."

TO THE

TRUSTEES* AND CONGREGATION

OF THE

AFRICAN CHURCH,

PHILADELPHIA.

BRETHREN,—

"Grace be to you, and peace from God our Father, and from the Lord Jesus Christ."

We could not, ourselves, have devised any words equally expressive, with the above, of a sincere Pastoral affection for you: and in the Spirit which they breathe, we make this

DEDICATION.

You will recollect those Holy Offices which you joined in, upon an important day; and the instruction which you listened to, before many witnesses.†

SAMUEL MAGAW,
JAMES ABERCROMBIE.

---

* The Trustees are, William Gray, Absalom Jones, William White, William Gardner, William Welcher, and Henry Stewart.

† The venerable Clergy of almost every denomination, and a number of other very respectable citizens were present.

TO THE PUBLIC.

The occasion on which the following Discourse was delivered, ought not to be deemed too inconsiderable for any farther notice. The opening of an *African Church* in *America;* and perhaps, *the first,* is a remarkable event in the progress of christian knowledge. At the request, therefore, of the people expressly concerned, and with the countenance of several most respectable characters, who wish well to them, the Author of this Discourse, assents now to its proceeding from the press. It was prepared in unavoidable haste, and under such peculiar circumstances of failure of health at the time, that it could not have been undertaken at all, or even tolerably executed, when undertaken, had it not been for *Dr. Rush's* distinguished attentions, and his most valuable hints, of which the Preacher was fortunate in availing himself.

The familiarity of the *style,* and plainness in the *manner* of address, it is to be presumed, require no apology.

ORDER
OF THE
SERVICE IN THE DESK.

1. Introductory Sentences.

"The Lord is in His holy Temple; let all the earth keep silence before Him." *Hab.* ii., 20.

"Thus saith the Lord; the Heaven is my Throne, and the Earth is my footstool: where is the house that ye build unto me; and where is the place of my rest?" *Isaiah* cxvi., 1.

"From the rising of the sun, even unto the going down of the same, my name shall be great among the Gentiles; and in every place incense shall be offered unto my name, and a pure offering: for my name shall be great among the Heathen, saith the Lord of Hosts." *Mal.* i., 11.

2. EXHORTATION.

3. THE GENERAL CONFESSION.

4. THE FOLLOWING PRAYER.

O Lord, our heavenly Father, almighty and everlasting God; Creator, Preserver, and Governor of the Universe; regard, we beseech thee, the prayers and praise we this day offer unto thy divine Majesty, in the place which we are now assembled in, to dedicate unto thee. Dwell in this house, we pray thee; accept and sanctify it, as an holy Temple, devoted to thy service, and to the maintenance of thy true religion and virtue. We know, O Lord, that thou dwellest not in Temples made with hands, so as to be circumscribed by them, as thou hast created the boundless expanse of Heaven for thy Throne, and the Earth outstretched, immense, for thy footstool; but whose Glory neither the boundless expanse of Heaven, which is thy Throne, nor the Earth outstretched, immense, which is thy footstool, nor even the Heaven of Heavens, are able to contain. Yet, though thy divine nature be thus unlimited, vouchsafe, we beseech thee, to be more especially present in this Sanctuary, by thy grace and heavenly benediction; that, as often as two or three are gathered together *here* in thy name, thou mayest be in the midst of them, to hear and to fulfil their petitions: so that this house may be forever sacred to the worship of thee, the only true God; where the Gospel of thy blessed Son, our Saviour Jesus Christ, may be faithfully preached, and the sacraments of his institution rightly and duly administered—that Gospel which is "the power of God unto salvation to as many as believe"—those holy Sacraments, which, being worthily received, are able to "nourish us unto eternal life."

And do thou, O merciful God, who before all Temples preferest a pure and upright heart, enlighten, preserve, convert us. "May thy Priests," *here* ministering before thee, "be clothed with righteousness, and may thy Saints, uttering their responses, sing with joyfulness." Pour out upon the whole Congregation a spirit of Piety and universal Charity; of that Piety which is fervent, yet humble—of that "Charity, which is the very bond of perfectness, the end of the commandment, and which proceedeth out of a pure heart, a good conscience, and faith unfeigned." May they ever possess a lively remembrance of the mercy thou hast vouchsafed unto them, in being graciously pleased to call them out of the darkness of Paganism, and the bondage of ignorance and error, into the clear light of Gospel Revelation, and "the glorious liberty of the children of God." May their understandings be evermore illuminated by that heavenly light, and may they ever "stand fast in that liberty wherewith Christ hath made them free."

May they so diligently learn the precepts of thy blessed Son, and so constantly follow his good example, that, having faithfully worshipped Thee in thy Church upon earth, they may, when the present period of their probation shall be accomplished, be admitted to the general assembly and Church of the first born in thy kingdom, where with Angels and Archangels, and all the innumerable Hosts of Heaven, they may laud and magnify thy glorious name, through the endless ages of eternity.

Hear us, O Lord, we humbly beseech thee, for the sake of thine only Son Jesus Christ, our Mediator and Redeemer, to whom, with the Father and the Holy Ghost, be all honor and glory, world without end. Amen.

5. The Morning Prayer continued.

6. Proper Psalms, 15, 84, 85, 122.

7. Lessons. { 1. Zachariah, 8th chap.
2. Colossians, 3rd chap.

8. Remainder of the Morning Service.

9. Part of the Communion Service.

10. The Collect.—*As for the first Sunday in Advent.* Epistle.—*Rom.* xiii., 8. For the Gospel, *Acts*, 11 to 27 v.

DISCOURSE.

"THE PEOPLE THAT WALKED IN DARKNESS HAVE SEEN A GREAT LIGHT."—*Isaiah* ix., 2.

As *I passed by*, soon after the walls of this building were carried up, *and beheld* the marble on the eastern front, *inscribed* with these words, my attention was exceedingly attracted by them; for I was struck with the propriety of such a *choice.* And, I know of none more suitable to direct our thoughts on the present interesting occasion. They relate to the Gentiles; and, this day, they have their accomplishment here.

Blessed God! who are these, *that gather themselves together?* They *come to thee!* They *come to thy light*, and *to the brightness of its rising. The sons of strangers do build up thy walls.* Their children's children *shall minister unto thee. In thy wrath didst thou smite them: but in thy favour hast thou had mercy on them.*

The style of holy Scripture is often figurative; and notices are taken from familiar objects, and circumstances generally known, in common life, in order to convey spiritual conceptions with all the greater clearness, and to render their impression the stronger and more abiding. This is remarkably seen in the writings of the sublime Isaiah. We have an instance of it before us, in the text,—where the words Darkness, and Light, which, literally, denote qualities universally understood, as they respect worldly things, are applied to certain qualities and conditions relative to spiritual things. "The people that walked in Darkness," is the Prophet's expression;—"The people" who lived in blindness and error, *have seen a great light*,—the light of the truth—the light of the glorious Gospel of Jesus Christ.

With some variation, how strongly is the same thought represented in the close of the verse—"they that dwell in the land of the shadow of death, upon them hath the light shined." Yes; of all darkness, that of the Soul is most dark: and of all who wander, the wanderers from the path of life, are most forlorn, and to be pitied. Of course, Divine illumination, the light from God, is, of all things, the most precious. *You* are a people who have "walked in Darkness." *You* who walked in darkness, have been favored with a change of that condition; you have been brought *to see* Light: And,

That Light is a glorious one—a *great* Light. From these considerations, do clearly flow certain duties, which eminently claim your observance.

I. You are a people who "have walked in darkness."

1. In being brought up as Pagans, or Heathen, unacquainted with Divine revelations, and the covenant of grace, *in your own country*.*

Your fathers, and some, perhaps, of you now present, did, near the shores of *Senegal* and *Gambia*,

---

* This is meant of the *general* state of the black people, or Africans.

on this or the other ill-fated range, or coast of *Africa*,—may be in *Benin, Congo*, or *Angola*,—ignorant of "God that made the world, and all things therein," bow down in adoration before stocks, stones, beasts, and the vilest creeping things,—pray to the hollow winds; or, dancing in wild circles, mutter to Devils;—or, in affrighted gaze, yell to the pale moon, to save you!—And it is known, that proportioned to the degrees of darkness, in the aforementioned respects,—especially the "gross darkness" covering the people,—must, of course, be the corrupt state of their manners.

2. You have "walked in darkness," as being slaves in *this country*—for slavery, and darkness, or ignorance, go hand in hand.

Can a poor African, dragged in fetters from his native land,—and here, driven and tormented under the lashes of cruelty, be any thing else than dark, —dark! Can a people, kept back from knowledge, expressly for this reason—lest it should unfit them for being beasts of burden,—*can they* be any other than dark?

To the credit of humanity, in *this* part of America, and several other parts, *such treatment* hath been held in abhorrence. It is unknown, except in narratives from abroad.

Still, at the very best, slavery is a hard allotment. It sinks the mind, no less than the body; weakens its capacity; destroys all *principle;* corrupts the feelings; prevents man from either discerning, or choosing aright in any thing. Yes, and in the proportion that it exists any where, it has its effect in vitiating the general manners.

PENNSYLVANIA! thou hast considered this. Thou hast mitigated its ills, in the first instance; and, in the most proper manner which the evil would admit of, art pursuing the plans for its entire abolition.

3. You "have walked in darkness" as *sinners.* In this respect, all mankind are upon a footing—they all *walk in darkness.* The term is fitly chosen, indeed, to express *the state of man.* He has lost sight of his chief end, and of the means to attain it. He mistakes his supreme good. He wanders in crooked paths. He exposes himself continually to dangers. He falls into innumerable vices and corruptions—and no wonder—for he walketh in darkness.

This darkness may be considered in a two-fold view,—as *external* and *internal.* The *external* darkness includes that state of things in the world, which is opposed to the knowledge of God, and true religion; those circumstances severally, or taken together, which the *Evil One* makes use of, as a medium, through which to carry on his own foul business. It comprehends all those erroneous systems of religion which prevailed among the different nations, before the appearing of the Messiah, Jesus Christ; and all the schemes or systems, whatever may be their names, that have been substituted for his religion since.

The *internal* darkness is seated in man's mind. It is an immoral disposition of the heart; a corrupt state of the affections. It is THE ENMITY AGAINST GOD, spoken of by St. Paul. It is that aching, wrathful abyss, (if I may so express it,) *void and without form*—till the Spirit of God "*moveth upon the face of it*," and saith, "Let there be light."

The depraved condition of the soul, being the dreadful effect of man's fall, you find set forth in holy Scripture, by no expression so frequent, as that of "Darkness." And, what is very observable —this internal darkness always implies that extreme evil, *Unbelief*—a distrust in the Almighty, and his declaration; and, in relation to the redemption offered to the world—it is a refusal to accept thereof, or to comply with its gracious terms.

II. In the next place, let us observe, agreeably to our text, that a "People that walked in darkness," *external* and *internal*, "have seen a great light." They have perceived by the eye of their understanding—they have discovered—they have become acquainted with that which will guide them to liberty and happiness.

By this "great light," is meant the knowledge of true religion—the instruction contained in the gospel of Jesus Christ; "the light of the glory of God in the face" of his beloved Son,—who is himself called "the light of men;" "the true light which lighteth every man that cometh into the world." Verily, under the circumstances in which this world lay by reason of sin, and, in the expectations of deliverance through the grace and virtue of a messenger sent from GOD, who is *the eternal essential light*, there could not be a more proper word summarily to characterize that divine messenger than LIGHT. Well, therefore, may the beautiful metaphor be used, as it often is, to designate or express *his influence.* This is called light, as opposed to darkness. It dispels darkness. It irradiates the external and internal hemispheres of the mind. It is that *spiritual* medium of sight, by which we *see* spiritually. It shows God to be what he is. Our altars need no more to have this inscription, TO THE UNKNOWN GOD.

It reveals his name, his nature, his perfections.

It shows man, as a creature, and a sinner. It shows him in a very different view from what he is disposed to consider himself, by the light of his reason. It discovers to him his littleness, his dependance on a superior, his depravity,—and withal, his utter inability to save himself. Particularly does it open *the way of salvation;* setting forth, in a manner most comfortable, most easy to be understood by people of all capacities—high or low,—that "God may be just, and yet the justifier of him who believeth in Jesus." It shows, that grace is the true spring of holiness: that divine pardon produces divine peace; and this peace to be inseparable from purity and virtue. It shows, moreover, all the social and relative duties; and points out the connection of each of them with the glory of God, and with general and individual happiness. Yes, my brethern,—and to complete the whole, it opens the divine abodes of existence in the world to come. It carries your hopes steadfast and sure, to the morning of that bright day, in the which, the redeemed ones shall put on immortality,—shall all meet one another, and meet the Lord;—when dignity and excellence that cannot now be uttered, shall be theirs forever.

III. It is called a *great* light. Let us enquire into the reasons of this epithet. It is *great*, both with respect to its *object*, its *origin*, and its *circumstances*.

1. Its object: Here indeed, there is not *one* only, but many; and, in the like multiplied view, may the origin be contemplated, together with the other particulars.

In regard to the first,—I shall try a moment to direct your attention to the principal of all. It is a *great* light, because it manifests to the world, the *Great Being*. The knowledge of God, or the religious impression of an intelligent, almighty *Cause* of all things,—"the rewarder of them that diligently seek him", is as *essential* to human happiness, as the breath we draw, is now to the human life. Man may exist without knowing God: but, existence merely, is not happiness. A sensibility on our part, of the relation we stand in to the infinitely great and good Creator, and of the duty flowing from that relation,—it is this that gives man his dignified place in the arrangement of the universe. Yet, it is too certain, to be disputed, that such knowledge or sensibility might, through human degeneracy and weakness, in a great measure, or altogether, become lost. It actually did so. What was the state of the world, in this respect, before the revelation of Gospel light? What hath been its state ever since, in places where that light has not reached? or in minds which refuse its friendly aid, under all the circumstances that appreciate and recommend it? One cannot give a more express, and at the same time, a more full answer to the above, than in these few scriptural words, "Having no hope and *without God.*"

The great light I am speaking of, immediately tends to the removing from human minds, that obscurity which covered them, with regard to that infinite Being. It is light that *doth make manifest.* And it is this *great* light that hath revealed or manifested God—*not in the mysteries of his nature*, but, as far, as by us, he may be known; a Being great and good; in whom the most entire confidence may be reposed; a Being who ordereth and governeth universally, and in the most perfect manner; a Being who is the standard of excellence; and who is still the compassionate benefactor of man though fallen; a Being who is reconciling the world unto himself; who is establishing an intercourse between earth and heaven; bestowing forgiveness through a Mediator; and opening all the springs of righteousness and consolation. Here there arises in view:

Another object of this light, enhancing its exalted nature and qualities; I mean the great salvation by the Gospel of Jesus Christ; a salvation from sin and death, into holiness and life eternal: for whereever its gracious influence is experienced, *there* peace is established; the dominion of Satan is overturned, and a new dominion fixed in the soul—the reign of God; new principles are implanted—the principles of light and love; a new life communicated—the life of heaven.

This sketch must suffice at present.

Other particulars, numerous and important, might here be brought forward, as *objects* of the *great light* before us; but, as the *principal* ones contemplated just now, do virtually include or refer to all the rest; I forthwith pass on,

2. To the greatness of this light, in respect to its *origin* or *sources*.

It is *great*,

(1.) Because it comes from the *Great* Being, "the Father of Lights," the Author and Creator of all things. He "who commanded light to shine out of darkness" *in the beginning,* hath now "shined into our hearts, to give us" this light.

(2.) Because it was conveyed to the world, by the *great* Immanuel, the son of God, "the brightness of the Father's glory, and the express delineation of his person;" of whom it was predicted, that "he should be great." It was conveyed by Him whose immense dignity, and divine attributes, attested and announced in the clearest manner, must give it value. It was conveyed by Him who was THE WORD and in the beginning "with God;"—"who hath a name above every name;" of whom it is said, as "the first begotten," "and let all the angels of God worship him;" and "thy throne, O God, is for ever and ever"—upon whose shoulder is "the government," as Mediator—the WONDERFUL,—the *Coun-*

sellor, the *Mighty God*,* the *Everlasting Father*,† the *Prince of Peace*—"able and willing to save unto the uttermost." I repeat it. This light, this "Wisdom which is from above," conveyed by Him must be *great*.

(3.) It is great, because it is communicated by the agency of the *Holy Spirit*, whose power is great to overcome all resistances from earth and hell; whose office it is to "reprove the world of sin, of righteousness, and of judgment;" the Spirit who led the disciple Peter, to make the memorable confession which his Lord entitles THIS ROCK, "on which he will build his church, and the gates of hell shall not prevail against it;" the Spirit through whose divine irradiations, the ancient prophets, and all the men of God from the beginning, saw, and foretold the several periods of the Messiah's Kingdom; its dawn, its commencement, its gradual unfolding, and the unutterable glory in which it is to issue; the Spirit, whose guidance and inspiration were given in a manner still more extraordinary, unto the Apostles, leading them unto all truth; bringing to their remembrance all that their Master had taught them; endowing them with miraculous powers; accompanying their preaching with irresistible energy and demonstration; instructing them how to answer and refute their adversaries; supporting them and their pious followers against the spirit and malice of the world; qualifying them severally

* The mighty Lord, or Heir of all things—Lord over all.

† The Father of the perpetual *age to come*, the age of the Gospel.

to fulfil the great purposes of the ministry; and abiding with all the faithful servants of Christ, ministers and people to the end of the world: the Spirit who is the author at first, and the promoter ever afterwards, of all saving impressions, gracious influences, and heavenly virtues in the human mind; the inspirer of the gifts of faith, of purity, of love, of consolation. Through his agency and operation, is this *light* communicated.

3. I said it is *great* in relation to the circumstances appertaining to it: and this is the third head, with which the consideration of the greatness of this light, supplies me.

(1.) It is *great*, because it hath endured a great while—from the fall of man to the present day. It is as old as the creation. With its early rays it comforted and refreshed the patriarchs. Increasing gradually, it was a guide to the prophets. From one age to another, down to the "fulness of the time," it taught the good and just to "live by faith." It was reflected back in hope and consolation, from every type and ordinance of the law. It encircled every altar. It interpreted every sacrifice. It enabled the members of the church of God, to look through each emblem and shadow, to the substance. In a word—it may be traced in a distinguishable stream, up to the beginning of time: it will extend down to the end of time; and it will shine more and more "unto the perfect day."

(2.) It is *great*, because it shall illuminate the whole world. Yes, "from the rising of the sun, unto the going down of the same," it will cause the name of the Messiah to be "great among the heathen." In a more eminent degree than we can have any just conception of, at present.

"One tide of glory, one unclouded blaze"—

shall cover the earth.

Innumerable passages of Scripture prove the future universal prevalence of this light: meanwhile, the happiest comparisons, and most expressive charming prospects are made use of often, to represent its excellency and increasing brightness.

I refer you, particularly to the Book of Psalms;—to the Prophets, Isaiah, Zachariah, and Malachi;—to the books of the holy Gospel, expressly so named; to the Epistles of St. Paul, and the Revelation of St John: the substance of their report is, that by the prevailing and expanding of this light, the "Dominion" of Christ, shall be from sea, even to sea; and from the rivers, even to the ends of the earth;* that every where, the walls of his church shall be called "salvation, and its gates praise;"† that "in every place, incense shall be offered to his name, and a pure offering;"‡ that the wilderness and solitary places shall be universally made glad, and the desert blossom as the rose;§ that the mountains shall exult, the vales be filled with melody; the trees of every forest break forth into singing;‖—the eyes of the blind be opened, and the ears of the deaf unstopped;"¶ that "the fulness of the Gentiles shall come, for the same Lord over all, is rich

* Psal. 72. † Isa. 60. ‡ Mal. 1.
§ Isa. 35: 1. ‖ Ch. 44. ¶ Ch. 29; Ch. 35.

unto all that call upon him;* that the ransomed of the Lord, shall return, and come to Zion with songs, and everlasting joy upon their heads;"† that '"a great multitude"—countless by men, "of all nations, and kindreds, and people, and tongues, shall stand before the throne, and before the Lamb, clothed in white robes, and palms in their hands‡"

(3.) Lastly, it is *great*, because, as it will shine on with unceasing lustre, until the end of time; so it will shine hereafter, in the glory which it produces throughout all eternity.

From the words thus opened and explained, there clearly arise certain duties, which you are expressly concerned in. Allow me with affectionate plainness to state and recommend them.

1. The first is Gratitude to God, for having directed, in his own wise Providence, that you should come from a land of Pagan darkness, to a land of Gospel light; from a state, afterwards, of slavery, to a state of liberty; and now, from guilt and sinfulness, to this state of salvation through our Lord Jesus Christ.

As for those who brought you, or your fathers, from your own country,—one may say of them, with a little variation, because of the different circumstances—as *Joseph* said to his brethren, "But as for you, ye thought evil against us; but God meant it unto good, to bring to pass, as it is this day, to save much people alive."

I am aware that your condition, or cases severally,

---

* Rom. 11. † Isa. 35. ‡ Rev. 7.

may differ a good deal, one from the other. I will specify an instance, and consider it with you, a moment; not losing sight of the gratitude just mentioned. As the greater number of you are free, so there may be others of you yet in bondage; these nevertheless, have received mercies enow to thank God for. His dispensations are unquestionably wise and proper. Whatever he permits, will turn to the real profit of such as do resign themselves to his good pleasure. Your present situation does not hinder you from being Christ's freemen. Your present situation gives you some advantages above what others have: yes, and very possibly, above what your masters have,—in that your humbleness of mind, your patience, faithfulness, and trust only in God, will add to the greatness of your future happiness.

2. The next duty is *gratitude* to your *earthly benefactors,* who planned your emancipation from slavery.

There are certain evils, which, when once they have obtained footing, and become *epidemic*, as it were, are scarcely seen as evils; no wonder then if they be slow and difficult to remove; so it hath been with slavery. A few humane, considerate persons, at an early period of our settlement in this country,—yes, in *Pennsylvania* particularly, were moved by the Divine Spirit, to open *light* upon this darkness. Their testimony was treated as visionary for a while; but, in time, it gained upon the judgment and consciences of men.

Here, you will recollect the names of LAY, of

WOOLMAN,—and above all, ANTHONY BENEZET;—whose labors were unwearied in your behalf; whose works of benevolence and love, have followed them to the regions of peace and blessedness beyond the grave.

There are also living characters not a few, in this city, and throughout the *United States,* heartily engaged in the same business of humanity. Behold, how intent they are to do your people good!

You owe much likewise, to those persons who planned schools for the instruction of your children.

This instruction is as the *door* introducing the young people to the *great light.* Knowledge is the best foundation for integrity and usefulness: and it is the element and life of *Freedom.*

You owe much to the Pennsylvania Society for promoting the abolition of slavery, and the relief of free negroes unlawfully held in bondage. The memory of *Franklin* here rises before you. He was its President. With the like views in which it originated, may it persevere, till its work be completed.

But especially, do you owe a large debt of gratitude to the citizens of Philadelphia, who assisted you by donations and loans, in the building of this handsome, spacious, and very convenient church.* You thought that to have an house of your own to assemble in for public worship, was, in consideration of your increased numbers, now desirable and expedient. In the same view have your patrons

---

* Dimensions, 60 feet, by 40—height proportional.

and friends regarded the matter, and countenanced your proceedings. And, as with brotherly kindness and complacency, they leave it to yourselves to fix upon, or adopt such system, order, and mode of worship as may be most agreeable to you; so have they found a perfect freedom in helping you to prepare a place, where that system, order, and mode may peacefully reside, and operate.

On the pleasing ground marked out above, I *could* go farther,—indulging *your* feelings,—and *my own*, by particularly mentioning some characters in this place, preeminent for generous actions, whenever they have opportunity; and who truly have been so, with regard to you:—But we are restrained in that satisfaction. There is, however, what will be infinitely more acceptable to them; namely, to see that their acts of kindness *do good.*

Most favorably assisted, the pious labor of your hands hath prospered thus far; and you are now happily assembled, for the first time, within these walls;—*we* offering our congratulations; and cheerfully uniting with *you* to worship the God of All.

3. Another duty, is compassionate love to your brethren, who are yet in darkness, or bondage, in other parts of the world. Be tenderly affectioned towards their condition. Pray publicly, and privately, that "the Lord may hear your voice, and look upon their affliction, and their labor, and their oppression."

O, mighty God! Thou dost encourage us in this thing. For notwithstanding the confusion of nations, and the corruption and madness of human passions, there is some prospect that the general cause of justice, of freedom, and of peace on earth, will at last prevail!

4. Humility is the next duty. Remember your former condition. Pride was not made for man, in any, even the highest stations in life; much less for persons who have just emerged from the lowest. It is said, there is a great deal of this among your people, already; and that it is increasing extremely fast. I wish this might be no more than a surmise: and then, that even the surmise itself might be dropped; for your friends meet with discouragements on this head. Will you, my brethren, guard against pride? Will you reflect on the nature of the evil itself; the offences that come by it; and other unhappy consequences!

It was a custom among the Jews, as you find recorded by Moses, in the book of Deuteronomy, ch. 26:5; when the Priest received the *Basket of first fruits* from them; for each person to declare, in the house and presence of the Lord, the history of the mean and wretched origin of his family: "A *Syrian* ready to perish, was my father."

In like manner, when you are tempted to cherish the least pride, in your freedom—in dress—in your favorable reception among your fellow-citizens, and even in this *stately building;* or in any of your civil, as well as religious privileges; then check yourselves, by confessing privately and publicly, that "a slave ready to perish, was my father:" or if all cannot say this; you may unite in expressions still more humbling, and say "a sinner—a fallen man—a rebel against God—an heir of wrath; and, until redeemed, a child of hell, *was my father*."

5. Circumspection in your conduct and intercourse with the world, is another duty that you are especially concerned in. "See that ye walk circumspectly; not as fools, but as wise." Remember, that you have enemies, as well as friends; that you will be narrowly watched; and that less allowance will be made for your failings, than for those of other people. This circumspection will be more necessary, as you have become a religious society.

Peaceableness among yourselves, and with all men, is indispensable to a fair character; as also truth in your dealings, in your words, and in your inner man; diligence in providing things honest: temperance and sobriety; an obliging, friendly, meek conversation.

Here a particular thought occurs to me, which is not to be suppressed: with regard to those of you who are *not free*, you must not be cast down, nor discontented. It is a dispensation of Providence, as I hinted already, to which you should submit in quietness, for conscience sake: and in so doing, you shall certainly meet with good. I give you St. Paul's advice, adapted exactly to your situation: "Let as many servants as are under the yoke, count their own masters worthy of all honor: that the name of God, and his doctrine be not blasphemed."*

---

* 1 Tim. vi., 1.

To proceed: You have built an house for the public worship of God; and this day, solemnly dedicated it unto Him.

O may the Lord our God accept of the dedication! Let Him not leave this people, nor forsake them! "Hear thou in Heaven, their prayers, and their supplications, and maintain their cause!"

Come then, ye people, highly favored! Your house is *Holiness unto the Lord!* Let none who ever worship in it, dishonor it at any time, or in any way. You have here, in the most public manner named the name of Christ, and told us, you "have seen His star in the east, and are come to worship Him;" depart then—depart from all—yea, even from the shadow of iniquity.

It is not a small matter, to have even heard of the true God. It is still a greater to have been taught His pure religion: But, together with the above—for *you* to be encouraged in the course of events to build a temple to that God, wherein His name may be adored—this is indeed *an honour* bestowed upon you. Here then, be assured, is a period in your progress and profession, which will prove very remarkable: For, according as your conduct henceforth turns out well or ill, your example will be a praise in the view of all around you, or a reproach. Yes, this very house, or rather, the conversation of those belonging to it, "is set for the fall or rising again of many"—of the people of *your colour.* On the right improvement of your present advantages, depends, perhaps, the fate of your brethren in bondage in every part of the world. Strengthen the hands of your friends every where by your pure and unexceptionable conduct. This will be to "let your light shine" in favour of the multitudes yet covered with darkness. This will be encouraging the deliverance of those who are bound.

A contrary behaviour will certainly increase their darkness, and tend only to rivet still closer their chains. It may render the yet existing reproach of your country perpetual.

To conclude—strive to escape from the darkness of sin. O let it not be "your condemnation, that light is come into the world, and that you have chosen darkness rather than light, because your deeds are evil." With your own eyes, behold the *great light* that has been described, and walk ye in it. Prize beyond all things the instructive, renovating grace of the Gospel. Reflect on the considerations now offered for that purpose. Attend, I beseech you, to the admonitions of your own consciences; to the calls of Providence; to the word of the Lord; to the teachings of the Divine Spirit; to the terrors of neglecting so great a salvation; to the hopes and joys of obtaining it; to the sure prospects of glory, honour, and immortality in the life to come.

Thus we have asked, O great God! for the counsel, and light, and Blessing we need. Thus, have we opened these doors, for Thy sacred worship, and to Thine honor. Thus, with Thy permission, have I spoken to this people whom we take by the hand as *Brethren* in Christ Jesus. Who can doubt, that Thou wilt look down from Heaven, and cast upon us the bright beams of Thy mercy?

My Respected Audience:

What if now, before we part, some free-will offering should be made in favour of this dedicated house. Prayers never come up more acceptably before God for a memorial than when united with alms. And I am inclined to believe, that there are very few occasions, if any, on which such an union could, with more propriety than the present, take place.

Under some difficulties, though highly favoured, —after considerable delay and apprehensions, at times, much greater, it hath pleased Providence to permit this goodly building to be brought on to its present state. There is more must be done to it yet, you see, ere it will be quite safe and convenient to assemble in, and very probably, notwithstanding the economy of the managers or trustees, a share of the past account is yet unpaid.

The people of the congregation may, by easy contributions from time to time, help themselves in this laudable business. Yes, and it may be reasonably expected, that each of you now present—I speak to those of the congregation—will, this day, give something for that purpose. And, for your encouragement, these respectable citizens, a number of your benefactors—your fellow-christians also—will cheerfully go on to encourage and assist you.

Will *you* then, (I address myself to such benefactors) will you allow me to solicit a present contribution in the generous view intimated above? and then we shall depart with satisfaction.

To press this matter much, is totally unnecessary: For, it has ever appeared to me a trait in the *Philadelphia* character, that the citizens looked not for *pressing solicitations* to do beneficent actions, but for opportunities.

"And God is not unrighteous, that he will forget your works and labor that proceedeth of love."

ACT OF INCORPORATION.

To all to whom these presents shall come:

Section First.

KNOW YE, that we, William Gray, Absalom Jones, William White, William Gardner, and Henry Stewart, by virtue of an Act of the Legislature of the Commonwealth of Pennsylvania, entitled "An Act to confer on certain Associations of the citizens of this Commonwealth the powers and immunities of Corporations or Bodies Politic in law," do hereby constitute and declare ourselves

8*

and our successors duly chosen, as are hereafter provided, for a corporation or body politic in law, to be known by the name of the Trustees of the African Episcopal Church of St. Thomas, in the city of Philadelphia, until Easter Monday, which will be in the year of our Lord one thousand seven hundred and ninety-six, and from and after the said day, by the name of the Minister, Church Wardens and Vestry-men of the African Episcopal Church of St. Thomas, in the city of Philadelphia.

Section Second.

And the election of the Minister, of the Church Wardens, and of the Vestry-men, who are to constitute the said corporate body, from and after Easter Monday, which will be in the year of our Lord one thousand seven hundred and ninety-six, shall be chosen from time to time by the members of the said church, agreeable to certain articles or rules by them made and entered into, on the twelfth day of July, in the year of our Lord one thousand seven hundred and ninety-four: And the said articles and rules are hereby declared to be binding on this corporation, and not to be altered by them in any respect.

Section Third.

That the said Minister, Church Wardens, and Vestry-men, and their successors, by the name and title aforesaid, shall for ever after be persons capable in law to purchase, have and receive, take, hold and enjoy, in fee simple, or of any lessor, estate or estates, any lands, tenements, rents, annuities, liberties, franchises, and other hereditaments, by the gift, grant, bargain, sale, alienation, enfeoffment, release, confirmation or devise of any person or persons, bodies politic or corporate, capable to make the same.

And further, that the said corporation may take and receive any sum or sums of money, and any kind, manner or portion of goods and chattels, that shall or may be given or bequeathed to the said Minister, Church Wardens and Vestry-men, and their successors, by any person or persons, bodies politic and corporate, capable of making a gift or bequest thereof; such money, goods and chattels to be laid out by them in a purchase or purchases of lands, tenements, messuages, houses, rents, annuities, or hereditaments, to them and their successors forever.

Section Fourth.

And the said Minister, Church Wardens, and Vestrymen, and their successors shall and may grant, alien, or otherwise dispose of any messuages, houses, lands, tenements, or hereditaments, other than the house of public worship, or church aforesaid, and the burial ground or grounds, which they now do or may hereafter possess as to them may seem meet and proper. *Provided always*, That in the disposition, sale, or alienation of such messuages, houses, lands, tenements, and hereditaments, the consent and concurrence of two-thirds of the

Vestrymen shall be had and obtained; and, also, the moneys arising from said disposition or sale be appropriated to the purchasing and procuring other more convenient messuages, houses, land or tenements as aforesaid, as the said vestry may deem proper and expedient, and to no other purpose whatever.

Section Fifth.

And the said Minister, Church Wardens, and Vestrymen, and their successors, or a majority of them, shall and may convene from time to time to make rules, by-laws, and ordinances, and transact every thing requisite for the good government and support of the said Church. *Provided always,* That the said rules, by-laws, and ordinances be not repugnant to the Constitution or laws of the United States, or to the Constitution and laws of this Commonwealth.

Section Sixth.

And the said Minister, Church Wardens, and Vestrymen, shall have full power and authority to make, have, and use one common seal, with such device or devices and inscriptions, as they shall think proper, and the same to break, change, alter, and renew, at their pleasure.

Section Seventh.

That the said Minister, Church Wardens, Vestrymen, and their successors, by the name aforesaid, shall be able and capable, in law, to sue and be sued, plead, and be impleaded, in any court or courts, before any judge or judges, justice or justices, in all manner of suits, complaints, causes, matters, and demands, of whatever kind, nature, or form they be, and all and every matter and thing thereunto do, in as full and effectual a manner, as any other person or persons, bodies politic, or corporate in this Commonwealth in like cases may or can do.

Section Eighth.

And until the appointment of the rector or principal minister of the said church, and afterwards, in case of death or removal of such minister, until any other minister shall be chosen agreeable to the usage and custom of the said church, the Church Wardens, for the time being, with the consent of a majority of the Vestrymen in vestry met, shall have the same powers and authorities relating to the disposition of the rents and revenues of the said corporation, as is herein before vested in the Minister, Church Wardens, and Vestrymen.

Section Ninth.

That the clear yearly value of the messuages, houses, lands, tenements, rents, annuities, or other hereditaments, the interest on the money by them lent, and the real estate of the said corporation shall not exceed the sum of five hundred pounds, money of Pennsylvania, exclusive of the moneys arising from the letting of pews belonging to the said church; and also, exclusive of the moneys arising from the opening of the ground for burials in the church-yard or yards belonging to the said church, which said money shall be received and disposed of by the Church Wardens and Vestrymen for the time being for the purposes herein before mentioned and directed.

In faith whereof, we have hereunto set our hands at Philadelphia, the second day of March, in the year of our Lord one thousand seven hundred and ninety-six.

William Gray,
Absalom Jones,
William Gardner,
Henry Stewart,
William White.

I have perused and examined the preceding instrument, and am of opinion, that the objects, articles, and conditions therein set forth and contained are lawful.

JARED INGERSOLL,
March 26, 1796. *Attorney General.*

We, the Justices of the Supreme Court of the Commonwealth of Pennsylvania, certify to his Excellency the Governor, that we have examined the preceding instrument of writing, and are of opinion that the objects, articles, and conditions therein set forth and contained are lawful.

As witness our hands,

THOMAS MCKEAN,
EDWARD SHIPPEN,
JASPER YATES,
THOMAS SMITH.

Philadelphia, March 28th, 1796.

[SEAL.] *In the name and by the authority of the Commonwealth of Pennsylvania, Thomas Mifflin Governor of the said Commonwealth: To Mathew Irwin, Esq., Master of the Rolls of Pennsylvania, sends Greeting.*

THOS. MIFFLIN.

WHEREAS, it has been duly certified to me by Jared Ingersoll, Esq., Attorney General of the Commonwealth, and by Thomas McKean, Esq., Chief Justice, and Edward Shippen, Jasper Yates, and Thomas Smith, Esquires, Justices of the Supreme Court of Pennsylvania, that they have respectively perused and examined the foregoing *Act* or *Instrument,* for the incorporation of the Ministers, Church Wardens, and Vestrymen of the African Episcopal Church of St. Thomas in the City of Philadelphia, " And that they concur in opinion, that the objects, articles, and conditions therein set forth and contained, are lawful." *Now, know ye*, that in pursuance of the Act of the General Assembly, in such case provided, I have transmitted the said act or instrument of incorporation unto you the said Mathew Irwin, Master of the Rolls aforesaid, hereby requiring you to enrol the same at the expense of the applicants, to the intent, that according to the objects, articles, and conditions therein set forth and contained, the parties may become and be a corporation, or body politic, and in fact to have continuance by the name, style, and title in the said instrument provided and declared.

Given under my hand and the great seal of the State, at Philadelphia, this Second day of April, in the year of our Lord, one thousand seven hundred and ninety-six, and of the Commonwealth, the twentieth.

By the Governor. A. J. DALLAS, Sec'ry.

Enrolled, in the rolls office, for the State of Pennsylvania, in Letter of Attorney Book, No. 6, page 14, &c.

Witness my Hand and Seal of Office, the 27th day of October, 1796.

[SEAL.] MATHEW IRWIN, M. A.

THE

CAUSES AND MOTIVES

FOR ESTABLISHING

ST. THOMAS'S AFRICAN CHURCH.

OF

PHILADELPHIA.

WHEREAS, a few of our race did in the NAME and FEAR of GOD, associate for the purpose of advancing our friends in a true knowledge of God, of true religion, and of the ways and means to restore our long lost race, to the dignity of men and of christians; and—

Whereas, God in mercy and wisdom, has exceeded our most sanguine wishes, in blessing our undertakings, for the above purposes, and has opened the hearts of our white brethren, to assist in our undertakings therein;—and

Whereas the light of the glorious gospel of God, our Saviour, has begun to shine into our hearts, who were strangers to the true and living God, and aliens to the commonwealth of this spiritual Israel; and having seen the dawn of the gospel day, we are zealously concerned for the gathering together our race into the sheep-fold of the great Shepherd and Bishop of our souls; and as we would earnestly desire to proceed in all our ways therein consistent with the word of God or the scriptures of the revelation of God's will, concerning us, and our salvation;—and

Whereas, through the various attempts we have made to promote our design, God has marked out our ways with blessings. And we are now encouraged through the grace and divine assistance of God opening the hearts of our white friends and brethren, to encourage us to arise out of the dust and shake ourselves, and throw off that servile fear, that the habit of oppression and bondage trained us up in. And in meekness and fear we would desire to walk in the liberty wherewith Christ has made us free. That following peace with all men, we may have our fruit unto holiness, and in the end, everlasting life.

And in order the more fully to accomplish the good purposes of God's will, and organize ourselves for the purpose of promoting the saving health of all, but more particularly our relatives, the people of color. We, after many consultations, and some years deliberation thereon, have gone forward to erect a house for the glory of God, and our mutual advantage to meet in for edification and social religious worship. And more particularly to keep an open door for those of our race, who may be induced to assemble with us, but would not attend divine worship in other places; and

Whereas, faith comes by hearing, and hearing by the word of God, we are the more encouraged thereto, believing God will bless our works and labors of love;—and

Whereas, for all the above purposes, it is needful

that we enter into, and forthwith establish some orderly, christian-like government and order of former usage in the Church of Christ; and, being desirous to avoid all appearance of evil, by self-conceitedness, or an intent to promote or establish any new human device among us.

Now be it known to all the world, and in all ages thereof, that we the founders and trustees of said house, did on Tuesday the twelfth day of August, in the year of our Lord, one thousand seven hundred and ninety-four,

RESOLVE AND DECREE,

To resign and conform ourselves to the Protestant Episcopal Church of North America.—And we dedicate ourselves to God, imploring his holy protection; and our house to the memory of St. Thomas, the Apostle, to be henceforward known and called by the name and title of *St. Thomas's African Episcopal Church of Philadelphia;* to be governed by us and our successors for ever as follows.

Given under our hands, this Twelfth day of August, 1794.

Founders and Trustees.
William Gray, Absalom Jones,
William White, William Gardner,
Henry Stewart, William Gray,
for
William Wiltshire.

THE CONSTITUTION.

THE CONSTITUTION.

WHEREAS, we the Founders and Trustees of the African Church of Philadelphia, did by our unanimous consent, at a general meeting held for the purpose, on Tuesday the twelfth day of August, 1794, decree, and consent, to commit all the ecclesiastical affairs of our church to the government of the Protestant Episcopal Church of North America, and to establish her creeds and articles of faith among us, as the governing system of our church for ever: and that the following rules shall be the binding constitution of our church for ever.

First.—All our ecclesiastical affairs are committed to the rule and authority of the Protestant Episcopal Church, to be by the Bishop and other officers of said Church and their successors, regulated as occasion may require: *Provided always*, that the general doctrines, and principles of worship of said church, shall continue as now professed in the same, and understood to be the rule or government of the same. *And provided further*, that we and our successors shall always retain within ourselves the power of choosing our minister and assistant minister, duly qualified to officiate according to the established rules and discipline of said church.

Secondly.—The mode of admitting an adult person, shall be by the approbation of the minister and the church wardens; they having obtained satisfactory proof of the zeal and integrity of, and also a good report, of him or her desiring to become a member.

Thirdly.—After the church is regularly organized, the mode of choosing officers for the church shall be by ballot. No person to have a vote except those who have been regularly admitted, and shall have been a member of the church twelve months preceding the election.

Fourthly.—The officers shall consist of a vestry of twenty men, two of whom shall be chosen by the vestry, to do the duty of church-wardens. The duty of the wardens and vestry to be what is defined and enforced by the Protestant Episcopal Church aforesaid; and all such officers shall be chosen, annually on every Easter Monday, or as soon as may be after. All elections to be held under the inspection of the two presiding church-wardens; and in case of absence of one or both of them, their place shall be supplied by the vestry; otherwise, the congregation shall nominate persons, members of the church, to act in the capacity the wardens ought to act in, on the occasion:—

And likewise there shall be two members of the congregation to be nominated by them to assist the wardens or their representatives, justly and truly to inspect such elections, and make a true return thereof to the congregation. But as we are now situated, we cannot do anything by way of election, until the second Easter Monday next ensuing. Therefore, we the founders and trustees, do agree, and bind ourselves to conduct the business of the church until then; that is to say, the providing a minister, inspecting the admission of members, and in all points discharging the duty of wardens and vestry to the best of our power.

Fifthly.—The duty of the vestry, is to attend to the interest and welfare of the church in all its temporal concerns, and in order to save unnecessary trouble to the vestry in general, the church-wardens shall have full power to transact the business of the church, between the several stated meetings of the vestry, which shall be monthly; and at every such meeting the church-wardens shall deliver their returns for the preceding month and particularly state their transactions during the same, respecting the church, to the vestry:—And so continue to do, unless in case of emergency. In all such cases, the clerk of the church, shall have orders to summon the vestry. But it is thought unnecessary to summon them to their stated monthly meetings. The vestry is empowered to receive all monies issuing to the church in all manner of ways whatsoever; and to make such repairs and improvement in the the church, as a majority of them may see necessary, and to keep in good order the yard, and all and every messuage, tenement and hereditament, that doth now, or hereafter may, belong to the church and congregation. They are also to regulate the minister and assistant minister's salary, and also, the salary of the clerk and sexton. They are to keep a regular account of the debits and credits of the church in a fair and clear manner in a book provided for the purpose; the state whereof, is to be presented to the congregation, when required by them; which book with every document, or thing of value belonging to the church they may be possessed of, they are to deliver to their successors, at their first meeting after their election.

Sixthly.—We ordain and decree, that none among us, but men of color, who are Africans, or the descendants of the African race, can elect, or be elected into any office among us, save that of a minister or assistant minister; and that no minister shall have a vote at our elections.

COUNCIL OF ADVICE AT BISHOP WHITE'S HOUSE.

"*Philadelphia, Sept. 9th,* 1794.

At a meeting of the Council of advice and standing Committee of the Convention of the Protestant Episcopal Church in Pennsylvania, in the Bishop's house.

PRESENT.

The Right Rev'd. Bishop White, and a quorum of the members.

The Bishop laid before the Council, the Constitution of the African Church of Philadelphia, a congregation of the people of color, who, having lately erected a building for the public worship of God, do now in consequence of free and mature deliberation, propose, and request to be associated with the Protestant Episcopal Church in the United States; and in particular to commit all their ecclesiastical affairs to the rule and authority of the Bishop and Church in this State of Pennsylvania.

The Bishop and Council are pleased with the application made as above, and are willing to accept the terms.

Resolved and declared therefore that as soon as the Trustees or Deputies of the said congregation, being duly authorized shall sign the Act of Association of the said church in this State, they shall be entitled to all the privileges of the other congregations of the Protestant Episcopal Church.

Agreed, that Dr. Samuel Magaw and Dr. Robert Blackwell, be a committee to meet the Trustees or Deputies of the African Church, and see them ratify the Act of Association.

Extract from the minutes,

SAMUEL MAGAW.

A member of the Council."

RECOMMENDATION OF A. JONES AS A CANDIDATE FOR ORDERS.

"To the Rt. Rev. Dr. William White and the Clergy, and Wardens of the Protestant Episcopal Churches of Philadelphia.

The Trustees and Representatives of the congregation of St. Thomas's Protestant Episcopal Church of Philadelphia, send greeting.

Whereas by grace a number of our race have formed ourselves into a congregation in Philadelphia, and on the 17th of July last, the house we prepared was opened and dedicated for divine worship, and whereas on Tuesday, August the 12th, 1794, at a special meeting held for the purpose, the Constitution of our Church was unanimously ratified upon the principles of the Protestant Episcopal Church of North America; and whereas on application to the Bishop and Clergy of the Protestant Episcopal Church of Philadelphia, we were graciously received into the bosom of the Church, on Sunday, 14th September, 1794; and on Sunday, October 12th, 1794, our being received into the fellowship and communion of the Protestant Episcopal Church of Philadelphia, was most cordially and fully announced from the pulpit by the Rev. Robert Blackwell; and whereas the several pastoral charges delivered to us by the Bishop, the Rev. Mr. Magaw, the Rev. Mr. Abercrombie, and the Rev. Robert Blackwell demonstrate the most affectionate and fatherly care for our spiritual and temporal progress and prosperity; and desiring to ornament our profession, and to walk worthy of the high privileges wherewith we are blessed, by a godly, sober, and exemplary life among men in general, but, more especially among our own color, in order to promote the gathering in of those who are wandering away from the paths of virtue and knowledge; we, after mature deliberation have concluded that it would be highly expedient to have among us a godly man of color, qualified to act as our Minister, knowing that it is derogatory to the discipline of the Church, to admit a Layman to exercise the functions of a minister.

With due deference to your wisdom, we presume to present to you our well-beloved brother, Absalom Jones, a man of good report, of Godly conversation, and zealously engaged in promoting religion and virtue among us, as a candidate for the above purpose. And in consideration of the utility of having such a person clothed with authority to visit the sick, attend funerals, administer the ordinances of baptism and the Lord's Supper, reproving, exhorting and following the wandering and careless to bring them into the sheepfold of Christ, and in view of the reverence and respect in which he is held by the generality of our color, and of his zeal for the prosperity of the church, and his assiduity in doing good for man: we, therefore, humbly hope that his want of the literary qualification required by the church, may, under our circumstances, be dispensed with.

Signed in behalf and by apointment of the congregation of St. Thomas's Church.

WM. GRAY,
WM. WHITE,
WM. GARDNER,
HENRY STEWART.
} *Trustees.*

Oct. 23d, 1794. The Council of Advice, and Standing Committee of the Convention of the Protestant Episcopal Church, met at Dr. Blackwell's on adjournment. Present, a quorum of clerical and lay members.

An address, or letter to the bishop and clergy of the Protestant Episcopal Church in Philadelphia, written in very respectful and affectionate terms, from the trustees and other representatives of the congregation of the African church, now called St. Thomas's Church, of Philadelphia, was laid before the Council, communicated through the hands of the bishop, representing among other things, that it would be expedient to have among themselves, a pious and duly qualified man of color, to discharge the functions of a minister, and recommending for the said purpose, as a candidate, Absalom Jones, a man of good report and Godly conversation. Whereupon, the Council being heartily disposed to favor the address and application as above, and entirely satisfied as far as doth to them appear, of the moral and religious character of the person recommended, do agree in opinion and respectfully advise that the most regular mode of proceeding is, for the Bishop to give his sanction and approbation to Absalom Jones, to officiate as a Reader of Divine service, &c., in the said church and a candidate for Deacon's orders, till the meeting of the convention of the church in this State, which will be in the month of May next. The 7th canon, ratified in General Convention, requiring with regard to the learning of those to be ordained that the requisition of an acquaintance with Latin and Greek, is only to be dispensed with by two-thirds of the Convention of the State to which the candidate belongs, and for good causes moving thereunto; the recommendation to the Bishop to the effect foregoing, to have the signature of the names of a majority of such Convention.

Extract from the book of Minutes.

SAMUEL MAGAW,
A member of the Council, &c., *Secretary*.

Oct. 22d, 1794. At a meeting of the Trustees and Representatives of St. Thomas's Church of Philadelphia, held in the Church—Present,

William Gardner,	James Dexter,
Doras Jennings,	Cyrus Porter,
William Gray,	Henry Steward,
William White,	Jno. Emory,
Cæsar Worthington,	Absalom Jones.

Absalom Jones reports that this day Bishop White informed him that a gentleman in Old England appropriated a part of his estate in Philadelphia, to a considerable amount, for supporting a free school for the African race and other good purposes, for their use and behoof, and desired that we should appoint a committee of our congregation to confer with him, and the Trustees appointed to act in conjunction with him on the business.

ACCEPTANCE OF THE CALL BY MR. A. JONES.

" *Oct.* 21, 1794.

To the Trustees of St. Thomas's Church.

Brethren—After some deliberation in my own mind upon the call you have given me, I sensibly feel that it is of such a serious nature as to cause me to tremble at the thought of such an undertaking. But, on my looking up to Him who is the Sovereign Ruler of all things, the recollection of Jacob's going over the brook unfurnished, with nothing but his staff and crook, and seeing what great things were done for him, and how his fears were banished, I was led to put my trust in God, and become your servant in Christ; and in all things begun, continued, and ended in his name, I hope He will be glorified, and our souls eternally profited.

*ABSALOM JONES."

"*Aug* 12*th*, 1795. At a meeting of the Trustees of St. Thomas's Church of Philadelphia, held in the Church on Wednesday,

Present—

Wm. Gray,	Absalom Jones,
James Dexter,	Jno. Henry,
Saml. Jackson,	C. Porter,
Rev. Dr. Magaw,	Rev. Dr. Andrews,
Rev. Dr. Blackwell,	Rev. Dr. Abercrombie.

This meeting was called by request of the Bishop, who presented an extract from the Journal of the Convention of the Episcopal Church of Pennsylvania, held in Christ Church, Philadelphia, June 2d, 1795, which was read and explained. The members present uniting with the restrictions therein specified, it was agreed to. The Bishop then informed the meeting that he could not with propriety ordain any person without being assured that the person so ordained would be supported by the Congregation that recommend him for Holy Orders.

---

* Mr. Jones—a candidate for Orders at the above date—was ordained Deacon by Bishop White in August, 1795. He was reported by Bishop White as Priest in 1804.

Resolved, That a support be provided for the minister ordained for St. Thomas's Church of Philadelphia.

Adjourned."

" Extract from the Journal of the Convention of the Episcopal Church of the State of Pennsylvania, held in Christ Church, Philadelphia, June 2, 1795.

It was moved and seconded, that the knowledge of the Greek and Latin languages, in the examination for Holy orders of Absalom Jones, a black man, belonging to the African Church of St. Thomas, in this city, be dispensed with, agreeably to the canon in such cases made and provided. Resolved, that the same be granted, provided, it is not to be understood to entitle the African Church, to send a Clergyman or Deputies to the Convention, or to interfere with the general government of the Episcopal Church, this condition being made in consideration of their peculiar circumstances *at present.*

JAMES ABERCROMBIE.
Secretary."

FIRST ELECTION FOR VESTRYMEN.

"We, the subscribers, being duly appointed judges of an election held in St. Thomas's Church, on Monday the 28th March, 1796, pursuant to notice given in the Church, and according to the Charter thereof, do certify that the following named persons are duly elected vestrymen for the ensuing year, viz.:

John Exeter, *Warden*,	Henry Stewart,
Charles Bunkam,	Samuel Jackson,
William Gray, *Warden*,	Robert Turner,
Ishmael Robins,	Joseph Williams,
Charles Golding,	William Thomas,
William Colston,	Rutland Moore,
Wm. Coleman, *Sec.*,	James Forten,
James Dexter,	Kent Burry,
Peter Mercer,	Jacob Gibbs,
Alexander James,	John Church,

John Emory, *Clerk of the Church.*

SAM'L BINGE,
ROWLAND PARRY,
JNO. J. PARRY,
WM. WIGGLESWORTH,
JNO. WOODSIDES, } *Judges.*

REGISTER OF THE MEMBERS UP TO 1794.

Rev. Absalom Jones, Wm. Gray, Wm. White, Wm. Wiltshire, Wm. Gardiner, Henry Stewart, Cæsar Worthington, James Dexter, John Henry, Dorus Jennings, S. Jackson, Cyrus Porter, Flora Madure, Joanna Patterson, Cæsar Thomas, Sarah Johnson, Henry Wilson, Ab. Ingles, Mark Reed, Tho's Batt, Cuffy Jordan, Molly Black, Harriette Reese, Hannah Kerney, Hannah Morris, Anthony Woodward, Ann Burk, Thomas Frederick, Rober Noble, Susan Groves, J. Doran, Katy Groves, Reuben Kinzey, Cato Wilks, Peter Bows, Hannah

Rowland, Francis Williams, Quam Butler, Cato Williams, Ruth Black, Rachel Groves, Tho's King, Tho's James, Rich'd Conner, Nathan Gray, George Vandyne, Rich'd Gray, Andrew James, Jesse Brown, Rob't Veneble, John Toge, John Kelly, Moses Anderson, Peter Robinson, Rob't Phillips, Rich'd Charles, Abm. Butler, Sawny Alexander, Moses Hocal, Joseph Robinson, Kingsly Williams, Jas. Brown, Jas. Williams, Wm. Harding, Alice Vandyne, Phœbe Cummings, Sarah Dexter, Margarette Cummings, Sylvia Brown, Diana Toga, Phœbe Kelly, Phœbe Eston, Hagar Parker, Rachael Coltiss, Nancy Coltiss, Rachel Anderson, Elizabeth Anderson, Sylvia Phillips, Mary Brown, Sarah Head, Temperance Richardson, Bella West, Sally Butler, Elenor Robinson, Rachel Gooden, Ann Harvey, Ann Brown, Katy Cox, Violet Brown, Ruth Harding, James Caton, Jehu Hall, Catherine Jackson, Jos. Pilgrim, Peter Richmond, Josh. Head, sen., Josh. Head, jr., Sharp Bickmore, Sam'l Reeves, Ed. Potts, Chas. Watt, James Lanty, David Stevens, John Jones, Ed. Ryan, Wm. Griffis, M. Mall, James Cross, Henry Duff, Chas. Thompson, Moses Oakley, James Potter, Kent Berry, Jas. Sparks, Cato Robinson, Joseph Parker, Dan'l Williams, Joseph Williams, William Coleman, Peter Mercer, Sam'l Harding, Jas. Williams, Jesse Brown, Alex. Hutchinson, David Dunkin, Frank Bacon, Cuff. Jordan, James Cole, sen., Joseph Scorer, Osburn Coleman, Devonshire Randall, Jno. Trested, Rich'd Williams, Elisha Miller, William Corentins, Sam'l Hall, Anthony Miller, Gregory Mulvin, Peter

Barns, John Coats, Jas. Harding, Jas. Gold, John Exeter, Benj. Woodby, Daniel Alexander, Lewis Weldon, Charles Cury, Cæsar Barns, Ed. Wood, Charles Bumkin, Cato Freeman, Philip Woodby, Charles Woodby, Frank Otoby, James Coleman, Sam'l Brown, Henry Wiltshire, Othello Pollard, Roderick Coleston, Joseph Tunch, Wm. Dickus, Richard Davis, sen., Richard Davis, jr., Cain Cuff, Moody Jackson, John Conner, Charles Weiden, John Church, Shandy Yard, James Burriss, James Foster, Thomas Williams, Peter Evans, William Campenfelt, Tatem Williams, Tony Hart, Robert Essex, James Forten, Benj. Johnson, John Richmond, sen., John Richmond, jr., Frank Johnson, John Sparks, Sam'l Jackson, Thomas Roderick, Tobias White, John Mills, Thos. Swan, Alexander Wetherhead, Joel Hazard, John Teebo, Jas. Barry, James Kinsey, Cæsar McCall, Benj. Moore, Philip Goodrich, Rob't Martin, Jacob Lawrence, William Scott, King William, Margarette Thomas, Philip Rixon, Favorout Bush, Mark Reed, Phillis Mann, Joanna Patterson, Diana Wills, Thos. Swan, Pleasant Swan, Eve Pompus, Jane Gray, Marilla Burk, Ann Styles, Jacob Warner, Mary Johnson, Isaac Jones, Charlotte Clarkson, Cherry Winchester, Eliza Weiden, Wm. Grubb, Diligent Dexter, Eliza Wright, Sarah Cole, Mary Black, John Emory, Margarette Woodby, Phillis Clark, Flora Madure, Elizabeth Jones, Ed. Wood, Rosanna Wood, Fanny Gray, Israel Burgo, Mary Warder, Mary Williams, Devonshire Craff, Amelia Harris, Ann Mercer, Wm. Thomas, Rob't Gordon, Simon Cato, Charles

Golden, Cato Jackson, Phœbe Seymore, Ann Brown, Jane Jacobs.—Total, 246.

In the year 1795, the names of persons recorded as members, in the aggregate, are four hundred and twenty-seven, almost twice the number of the preceding year. In addition to the regular members of the Church, we may reasonably suppose that a floating congregation of at least a hundred or more persons were attracted thither from various motives, thus filling it to its utmost capacity. For St. Thomas's at that time, was THE African Church. There were none, then, of the same class, to emulate her noble example, excepting the small company collected together in the blacksmith shop, fitted up for a place of worship by the venerable Richard Allen, aided by the active benevolence of a Christian community. This frame building, from all that we have learned, could scarcely seat one hundred and fifty persons.

SCHOOL ESTABLISHED.

In 1804, a day school for the instruction of youth was established by the Vestry, to be under their direction and control. They appointed a board of eleven trustees, eight of whom were selected from their own body, and three from the congregation. The duty of this board was to visit the school once in every month, to examine the scholars, note the progress made by them in their studies, and propose such improvements to the Vestry, in regard to the order and government of the school, as they might deem advisable. Each member of this educational society was required to pay into the hands of either of the trustees the sum of one dollar annually. The Bishop, or any of his Council, had the prerogative of visiting the school, and of proposing amendments to existing regulations. All proposed amendments were reported by the trustees to the Vestry at their ensuing monthly meeting.

The following named persons constituted the Board of Trustees appointed by the Vestry:

Robert Gordon,	Wm. Gray,
Cato Collins,	James Forten,
James Harding,	Randall Shepherd,
Robt. Douglass,	Wm. Thomas,
Peter Richmond,	Joseph Randolph,

Jno. Bowers.

FACTS CONCERNING THE CHARITY OF THE REV. DR. BRAY.

The Board of Trustees continued to manage the concerns of the school up to the year 1816; beyond which time no minutes of their proceedings appear. One fact in connexion, worthy of notice, is, that the expense of instructing ten male scholars was paid from the trust of the Rev. Dr. Bray. It appears that the Vestry finally gave up the control of the school and placed it in the hands of Solomon Clarkson (one of its members), who also, for a considerable number of years afterwards, was paid from the same charity for the tuition of the aforesaid number of scholars. Besides, there was a female school, taught by Madam Hand, in the Northern Liberties, supported from the same source.

"This ancient charity originated with the Rev. Dr. Bray, American missionary, the Bishop of London, and Mr. D'Alone, secretary to King William. In 1774, the ground rents of a large lot in this city were set apart for the payment of the expenses of two schools for blacks, one for each sex, to be educated gratuitously. 'The Associates' in England are perpetual; and from their appointments, three of our citizens, churchmen, constantly serve the schools as directors and governors. Those lately in service were Wm. Meredith, Thos. Hale, and James S. Smith, Esquires." *

For the last fifteen years, at least, this charity has been turned in some other direction. It has been ascertained that ever since the suspension of the schools here, the nett sum of *nine hundred dollars*, arising from said ground rents, has been forwarded to London annually.

We have been in communication with the "Associates" in England, through their Secretary, respecting the ground taken for suspending said schools, and have recently received in replication a polite note, from which is taken the following extract:—"The trust to which you allude is for the support of schools in British America. The 'Associates' have always been advised that the term 'British America' is to be construed as comprising the territory now known by that name, and not the territory which was so considered prior to the Peace of 1783, and that it is their duty to apply the trust accordingly."

* Watson's Annals, 2d vol., page 263. Ed. of 1854.

SOCIETY FOR SUPPRESSING VICE AND IMMORALITY.

In 1809 a Society was formed by the leading colored men of that day, for the suppression of vice and immorality among their people, composed of members belonging to different denominations of Christians. A tolerably correct idea of their plan of operations may be obtained from the perusal of the following copy of an appeal (from the original) to the Chief Justices of Pennsylvania, and the city and county of Philadelphia, for their approbation of the work in which they were about to engage.

PETITION.

* "*To the Honorable William Tilghman, Esq., Chief Justice of the State of Pennsylvania.*

A number of the free people of color have associated themselves together in a society by the name, title and description of the African Society, for the suppression of vice and immorality, among the people of our own race. They have for a long time viewed with a painful anxiety, the multiplied evils that have occurred and do daily occur, for the want of such advice and instruction as they feel desirous of giving, by visiting some of the more dissipated parts of the city and suburbs, on proper occasions, and using such persuasive measures as may be best calculated to produce reformation of manners among them. They, therefore, solicit

* A similar appeal is addressed also to the "Chief Justice of the city and county of Philadelphia."

your Honor's approbation and concurrence, in behalf of the society.

JON. TRUSTY, *Chairman.*

Philadelphia, 1*st Nov.* 1809."

Appended to this appeal, are commendations of the enterprise, in the hand-writing of some of the most illustrious persons, that graced the age in which they lived. We regard them as precious relics—mementos of friends in the olden times, which should not lie buried in oblivion. It is, therefore, with grateful pleasure, we proceed to transcribe them.

"I have read the Articles of the African Association and approve of them. The object is highly commendable, and there is reason to hope that the Association may produce very beneficial effects.

WM. TILGHMAN.

Philadelphia, Nov. 3, 1809."

"I have also read the Articles of the African Association, and heartily concur with the Chief Justice in the opinion above expressed.

B. FRANKLIN.

Philadelphia, Nov. 3, 1809."

"Every rational plan, to reform the people of colour, will always have my approbation. The effort now proposed to be made, by means of religious instruction and conversation, at seasonable times, has, therefore, my cordial wishes for its success.

JACOB RUSH.

Nov. 2, 1809.

By a certain financial arrangement, truly benevolent, of William Bradford, Esq., made before his death in 1793, between Dr. Benj. Rush, and Bishop White, St. Thomas' Church, became in possession of the Parsonage, situated in Powell street, between Fifth and Sixth, Spruce and Pine streets, in the year of our Lord 1809. It is a double three story brick building. The lot on which it stands, contains in breadth 16 feet 6 inches, and in length or depth 66 feet 9 inches, subject to an annual ground rent of thirty-four dollars. As a small testimony of profound gratitude, the Vestry had placed in front of the Parsonage, a marble slab with the following inscription:

"THE LEGACY OF WM. BRADFORD, ESQ.,
AUG. 19TH, 1793,
TO THE AFRICAN CHURCH OF ST. THOMAS."

TEMPORARY DIVISION IN THE CHURCH.

In the month of July, 1810, the noise of an angry tumult began to be heard within the borders of this interesting branch of the Church. It appears that certain disaffected members took upon themselves the responsibility of opening a communication with Mr. Alexander Cook Summers, (a colored gentleman of Jamaica,) respecting his becoming a candidate for the ministry in St. Thomas' Church. Such were the encouragements held out to Mr. Summers by those persons, that he was induced to leave his native home and embark for Philadelphia. On his arrival, he handed the letter which had been written to him, to Mr. Jones, who presented the same at a regular meeting of the vestry. The vestry, upon hearing its contents, expressed their indignant surprise at the course which had been thus pursued, and disavowed all connexion with, or participation in, the matter whatsoever. They accordingly appointed a committee to wait upon the Bishop for his counsel and advice, in relation to, what they conceived to be, a wicked attempt to create a division in the church. The Bishop, after hearing a statement of the case, recommended that an interview, if possible, be had between the Vestry and Mr. Summers. This proposal was accordingly made to Mr. Summers, by a committee appointed for the purpose, but he,—perhaps through the controlling influence of his friends—"absolutely refused" compliance with said proposal.

This sad occurrence developed a party spirit in the congregation which was not healed during the few remaining years that were left to the life of the Rector, or indeed for many years after his decease. Those discontented members finally seceded, hired a room in Zane street, employed Mr. Summers as Lay Reader, with the view of having him in due time ordained. Their expectations, in regard to increasing numbers rallying around them, were not realized. They struggled on, however, for a year or more; at the expiration of which time, they became wearied of the increased burden of taxation; which had the double effect of moderating their zeal in the ill-conceived enterprize, and of opening their eyes to their inexcusable folly and wrong doing.

What a lamentable picture did those days present to the truly pious mind! The Grand Adversary of God and man then waved in triumph his hellish banner of "envy, hatred, malice and all uncharitableness" within the sacred precincts, where love, unanimity, peace and concord should ever dwell. "The ways of Zion," then mourned, because few went up "to the solemn feasts" with duly prepared hearts. The Priests, the Ministers of the Lord, then wept "betweeen the porch and the altar, saying, SPARE THY PEOPLE, O LORD, AND GIVE NOT THINE HERITAGE TO REPROACH." How important is it for christians at all times to give heed to the admonition—"PRAY FOR THE PEACE OF JERUSALEM."

S. CLARKSON, PROPOSED AS AN ASSISTANT.

March 13th, 1811. Solomon Clarkson, by a resolution of the vestry was taken up to be educated for the ministry; and, in the event of success in the prosecution of his studies—no other impediment being in the way—he was to be received as an Assistant Minister to the Pastor then in charge. All this was sanctioned by the Minister, Vestry, and Congregation. They, by voluntary subscriptions, met the expenses of his board and tuition for a considerable time; but finding in the end, that he gave such poor promise of reaching a point of literary respectability, within any reasonable period, they advised him to abandon the idea of the ministry and seek some other calling. He soon afterwards commenced keeping a common day school, in which occupation he continued, until the day of his sickness, which terminated in death. Mr. C— was a godly man, warmly attached to the church, but was regarded as being very singular in his manners. He was communicative to few, except his confidential friends. He seemed to take pains to avoid the company of all others. He was very quick in his movements; in debate, rapid in the expression of his sentiments, but would never publicly oppose his friends though differing in opinion from them. Had he entered the ministry, he would, I am sure, have belonged to that class of ministers, whose sermons are always enveloped in "the blue blazes of hell fire and brimstone." One prominent trait in the character of Mr. C——, worthy of being imitated, was his punctuality. For twenty years or more, he acted as Secretary of the Vestry, and I always found him among the first in attendance. It was his uniform practice to read the Lessons, Epistle and Gospel for the day, at the church, before the time arrived for commencing divine service.

SKETCH OF THE REV. ABSALOM JONES.

The Rev. Absalom Jones, after having been actively and faithfully engaged in the service of the Church for the space of twenty-two years, was released from his anxious toils, and arduous labors, by the welcome messenger, Death—" gathered unto" his "fathers in the communion of the

Catholic Church; in the confidence of a certain faith; in the comfort of a reasonable, religious and holy hope; in favor with God, and in perfect charity with the world." He was born a slave; his young ideas, therefore, were never taught how to shoot forth their rays of intellectual light and beauty. He had arrived at manhood before he was initiated into the first branches of a common school education. He became somewhat proficient in these, by dint of self-application, during intervals from his secular labors. By industry, frugality, and economy, previous to his entering the ministry, he had accumulated some means which he invested in real estate. He was the owner of several neat dwellings, the value of which we have not ascertained. A day school was taught by him while he pursued a course of preparation for the ministry, and also for some time after he entered upon its duties and responsibilities. When he took charge of the church he was in the 49th year of his age.

The following narrative is copied from the original manuscript written by himself:

"I, Absalom Jones was born in Sussex," DEL., "on the 6th of November, 1746. I was small, when my master took me from the field to wait and attend on him in the house; and being very fond of learning, I was careful to save the pennies that were given me by the ladies and gentlemen from time to time. I soon bought myself a primer, and begged to be taught by any body that I found able and willing to give me the least instruction.

Soon after this, I was able to purchase a spelling book; for as my money increased, I supplied myself with books, among others, a Testament. For, fondness for books, gave me little or no time for the amusements that took up the leisure hours of my companions. By this course I became singular, and escaped many evils, and also saved my money

In the year 1762, my mother, five brothers and a sister were sold, and I was brought to the city of Philadelphia with my master. My employment in this city was to wait in the store, pack up, and carry out goods. In this situation, I had an opportunity, with the clerk, to get copies set for me; so that I was soon able to write to my mother and brothers, with my own hand. My spelling is bad for want of proper schooling.

In the year 1766, I asked my master the liberty of going one quarter to night-school, which he granted. I had a great desire to learn Arithmetic. In that quarter, I learned Addition, Troy weight, Subtraction, Apothecaries' weight, Practical Multiplication, Practical Division, and Reduction.

In the year 1770, I married a wife, who was a slave. I soon after proposed to purchase her freedom. To this her mistress agreed, for the sum of forty pounds. Not having the money in hand, I got an appeal drawn, and John Thomas, my father-in-law, and I called upon some of the principal Friends of this city. From some we borrowed, and from others we received donations. In this way we soon raised thirty pounds of the money, her mistress, Sarah King, forgiving the balance of ten pounds. By this time, my master's family was increased, and I was much hurried in my servitude. However, I took a house, and for seven years, made it my business to work until twelve or one o'clock at night, to assist my wife in obtaining a livelihood, and to pay the money that was borrowed to purchase her freedom. This being fully accomplished, and having a little money in hand, I made application to my master, in the year 1778, to purchase my own freedom; but, as this was not granted, I fortunately met with a small house and lot of ground, to be sold for one hundred and fifty pounds, continental money. Having laid by some hard money, I sold it for continental, and purchased the lot. My desire for freedom increased, as I knew that while I was a slave, my house and lot might be taken as the property of my master. This induced me to make many applications to him for liberty to purchase my freedom; and on the first of October, 1784, he generously gave me a manumission. I have ever since continued in his service at good wages, and I still find it my duty, both late and early, to be industrious to improve the little estate that a kind Providence has put in my hands.

Since my freedom, I have built a couple of small houses on the same lot, which now let for twenty-two pounds a year."

Mr. Jones, is said to have been very earnest and impressive in his style of preaching; but, it was never thought that his *forte* was in the pulpit. It was his mild and easy manners, his eveness of temper, his repeated visitations among the people, especially the sick of his flock, his active cooperation with every effort put forth for the advancement of his race,—(in which respects he had no superior among the contemporaries identified with him)—that endeared him to all who knew him. He was of medium height, dark complexion, with a stout frame, bland and open countenance, yet indicative of firmness. The costume among the Clergy of his day, was a black dress coat, breeches and vest of the same color, with top boots, or shoes with buckles, and black stockings, depending upon the season of the year. Mr. Jones, uniformly appeared in public, habited in the same manner.

His mortal remains now repose beneath the shadow of the church, which, under God, he was chiefly instrumental in founding, with the following epitaph upon his tomb:

TO THE MEMORY
OF THE
REV. ABSALOM JONES,

who, born a slave, and becoming possessed of freedom by good conduct, and rendered respectable by a course of virtuous industry, was principally instrumental in founding the African Church of St. Thomas, in which he was the first Pastor; and after discharging the duties of the ministry faithfully during 22 years, he departed this life February 13th, 1818, aged 71 years, 3 months, and 3 days.

BAPTISMS—INTERMENTS.

By reference to the Baptismal Record, I find the number of adults baptized between the years of 1796 and 1818 to be . . . 268

Infant baptisms, . . .	927—Total	1195
Confirmations, ...		274
Interments, ...		624

This may justly be regarded as a large number of interments in proportion to the size of the Congregation; but it may be accounted for from the fact, that other persons, besides members of the church, availed themselves of the privilege of burying their friends in the church-yard, by submitting to the payment of one-third more than was exacted of the members.

PRINCE SAUNDERS.

During the four years immediately succeeding the departure of the Rev. A. Jones, St. Thomas's was without any settled minister. Bishop White, the Reverend Drs. Magaw, Abercrombie, and Blackwell, when convenient, kindly supplied the pulpit by turns. Mr. Cato Collins, a very worthy man, and highly esteemed, in the absence of a clergyman—acted as Lay Reader, to which office he had been previously appointed.

In the month of June, 1819, Mr. Prince Saunders, from his great popularity among the people, bid fair for a while to be received as a candidate for Holy Orders in the Church. He had commendatory letters in his possession from persons of high distinction in London, showing how highly he was estimated there, for his gentlemanly bearing and fine scholarship. He was said to be of pure African blood, unprepossessing in his external appearance, but of highly polished manners and of brilliant parts. He was born in this country, but his uncommon brightness, while a youth, drew the attention of some influential and wealthy friend, who, as an experiment, had him sent to England to be educated; and the proficiency he there made, more than met the most sanguine expectations of his friends.

Mr. Saunders served the church as a Lay Reader for several months, and just as he was on the eve of being recommended by the Vestry to the Bishop as a Candidate for Orders, a grave charge was preferred against him from Hayti, which was not satisfactorily answered; and the lamentable result was, his dismissal from all connexion with the Church.

RUSSEL PAROTT.

January 28th, 1822. Mr. Russel Parott, a regular communicant member of the church, and a very talented young man, was, by a resolution of the Vestry—chairman giving the casting vote—taken up as a suitable person to be recommended as a Candidate for Orders. He was licensed as Lay reader by the Bishop in the following month. But this selection failed to give the general satisfaction to the congregation, desired. Hence, with a view of restoring harmony in the church, a resolution was passed by the Vestry at a regular stated meeting, held April 20th, 1822, to release Mr. P—— from any further obligation to serve them in the capacity of a Reader. This promising young man died August 3rd, 1824. As a tribute to his memory, a Society, styled the "Sons of St. Thomas," (two others co-operating,) had erected at the head of his grave, now in the church-yard, a monumental slab with the following inscription:

"In this grave is deposited the body of Russel Parott, a man of unblemished reputation, of pure morals, and of unaffected piety. He was, at the time of his decease, engaged in the study of Divinity, and a candidate for Holy Orders in the Protestant Episcopal Church.

He departed this life Aug. 3rd, 1824, aged 33 years, 9 mo., and 22 days.

In testimony of respect for his virtues and his talents, this memorial is erected by the Sons of St. Thomas, the Daughters of St. Thomas and the Female Baptist Assistance Societies, of the first of which he was a member, and of the two others a Director.

REVERENDS J. WILTBANK—J. GLOUCESTER.

March 20th, 1822. The Vestry succeeded in obtaining the clerical services of the Rev. James Wiltbank, who continued in the faithful performance of his pastoral duties up to the month of February, 1825, at which time he resigned, and accepted a call to the rectorship of St. Matthew's Church, Francisville. Mr. Wiltbank, at the time of his death, was a Chaplain in the U. S. Navy.

April 25th, 1825. The corporate body of St. Thomas's—adhering to the prevading import and spirit of their Charter, in their persevering endeavors, to secure if possible, a minister of their own race—put forth another effort in that direction in favor of the Rev. Jeremiah Gloucester, a colored clergyman of the Presbyterian denomination. But, difficulties were soon thrown in the way by certain ill-disposed persons, who concocted and preferred serious charges against him; whereupon a committee was appointed by the Corporation to institute an investigation of the matter. This investigation resulted in an honorable acquittal by the Presbytery of which he was a member. The Vestry continued in communication with Mr. G., up to the month of September following, but without reaching the desired result, and so the matter ended.

REV. P. VAN PELT.

In the Summer of 1826, the Rev. P. Van Pelt, a Presbyter of South Carolina, and in charge of one of the most important Parishes of that Diocese, visited the City of Philadelphia. During his stay here, he frequently officiated for our people, and much to their satisfaction and benefit. Previous to his return to the South, the Vestry of St. Thomas's Church tendered him a unanimous invitation to become their Rector. Bishop White, Dr. Abercrombie, and others of the City Clergy, knowing the desire of the congregation to secure his services, and believing that they would be productive of great good, strongly urged his acceptance of the call. To this, regarding it as a duty, he, at length, assented; but, in consequence of previous engagements at the South, did not enter upon his duties, as Rector, until June, 1827. Having been appointed Secretary of the "Domestic and Foreign Missionary Society," and editor of its Periodical, he resigned in October, 1830. On the eve of separating, the congregation, as a testimony of their affectionate regard gard, presented him, in addition to other substantial memorials, a large and beautiful silver pitcher. Mr. Van Pelt was a young gentleman of very prepossessing appearance, fine talents, and oratorical powers of a high order. During the three years of his ministrations he was very successful, through the divine blessing upon his labors, in promoting true and vital godliness among the people of his charge.

In 1829 he presented to Bishop White, *forty-four persons* for confirmation. The Sunday school rapidly grew in its dimensions, and greatly flourished. Its fame spread among the colored people of other denominations, from among whom large accessions were made to the school, they having at that time no Sunday Schools of their own. An organ, for the first time, was introduced into the Church, at his suggestion. Mr. V. P. evidently made an indelible impression upon the congregation of St. Thomas. The elder members of that time have since departed this life; but, I never knew them speak of the days referred to, unless in the most glowing terms, as pleasing reminiscences of the past. And I feel confident, that it is not possible now for me to introduce into the pulpit a clergyman more acceptable to our hearers—excepting our venerable and beloved Bishop—than the Rev. P. Van Pelt, D.D.*

REV. J. M. DOUGLASS.

In February, 1831, the Rev. Jacob M. Douglass,† accepted a call to the pastoral charge of the Church, and resigned the 17th of August, 1834. The present incumbent assumed the said post of duty September 17th of the same year.

Mr. J. M. Douglass was universally beloved for his suavity of manners, his eveness of temper, his kindly affections, his concern for the poor and needy, and for his earnest, impressive and pathetic discourses. He was evidently a man of that peculiar temperament which enabled him, under God, to calm the waters of strife and confusion that might threaten to make inroads upon the peace and godly quietness of the flock. For at the time of his resignation, the perfect unanimity, peace, harmony and concord that universally prevailed in the Church, marked the period as a happy era in its history, contrasted with the stormy days of the past. The present Rector, as he then with much fear and trembling entered upon the solemn duties of his station, having learned that this was the state of affairs among his people, sensibly felt the sooth-

* Dr. Van Pelt, is at this date, Professor of Oriental Languages in the Theological Department of Burlington College, N. J., and Secretary of the "Board of Missions of the Protestant Episcopal Church in the United States of America."

† He is now (1861) Rector of Zion Church, Philadelphia.

ing effect of the truth embodied in the beautiful line:

"He tempers the wind to the shorn lamb."

Having now arrived at the proposed end of a pleasant journey, and sketched, as we passed along, the history of St. Thomas's Church, through successive scenes of light and shadows, up to the date of our earliest pastoral connection thereto, we consider this a proper point from which to offer a few words to our parishioners, inciting gratitude for the past, hope and zeal for the future.

At this interesting period of time, a goodly number of those who witnessed the first opening services of this church, were still on the stage of action, still striving together with their wonted zeal for the interest of their beloved Zion, though fast ripening for the grave, as their hoary locks proclaimed. The affectionate recollection of them is still so fresh upon my mind, that I fancy them all to be now present before me, listening to the following address to their successors.

MY BELOVED BRETHREN:—In taking only a slight survey of the inheritance that has come down to us through the toils and labors of our venerable predecessors, we are instinctively led to sympathise with the Psalmist, and with grateful emotions exclaim—"THE LINES ARE FALLEN UNTO US IN PLEASANT PLACES; YEA, WE HAVE A GOODLY HERITAGE."

I would have you to mark well the following language used by the founders of this church:

"Being desirous," they say, "of avoiding all appearance of evil by self-conceitedness, or an intent to promote, or establish any new human device, they entered into, and established an orderly, christian-like government and order of former usage in the Church of Christ." They desired nothing more or less than to become a branch of the one Holy, Catholic, and Apostolic "Church; in which the pure word of God is preached, and the sacraments duly ministered according to Christ's ordinance, in all those things that of necessity are requisite to the same." For this exhibition of practical wisdom on their part, we should rejoice, and be thankful. It is not the boast of St. Thomas, that the mass of our people has hitherto been won to her standard. Yet it cannot be successfully denied, that she has exerted a powerful influence for good, among other denominations of her brethren, since organized into religious bodies. Whatever of taste, order and intelligence be now discovered among the various colored churches here, may in a great degree be traced to the stimulating influence of St. Thomas's. She stood alone, at one time, in favor of the education of the ministry and people. But a favorable change is now universally taking place. She was once spoken of in disparaging terms on account of her care for cleanliness and decency in the house of worship, her carpeted aisles, her pews and organ. But now, she is closely imitated in all these respects. I repeat, that it is not our boast that the mass have flocked to our Zion. The time has not yet arrived. It should be remembered, that though our people are rapidly improving, they are not yet fully developed. Our sober, rational, and inimitable devotional service, the Lessons, Epistles, and Gospels statedly read, are what they actually *need* in order to raise them to the dignity of intelligent christians; but, they are not as yet generally prepared to appreciate them, owing to their early prepossessions. But the day is at hand, when, from previous intellectual training, the rising generation will be fully competent, and every way disposed, to investigate matters closely. They will no longer be governed, as too many of their elders are now, by superstitious notions, false premises, and illogical conclusions. They will become honest and candid searchers after the truth. Then, the time will have arrived for St. Thomas' to arise in her strength, and make an aggressive movement—to challenge her brethren of other names to compare notes with her in regard to the basis of their ecclesiastical structures. It may be replied, that, in order to make aggressions, it is necessary to be armed with pecuniary strength, as well as spiritual vigor. Very true; but our reference is to future operations. At present, she looks occasionally to Head-quarters for material reinforcements, and I am happy to say, that she looks not in vain. But this is regarded as a temporary, not a fixed policy. Take a leisure walk, about the outer courts of your Zion; "mark well her bulwarks;" see the masked batteries, ready to open and do good execution in the future. Sixty years ago, your church edifice, stood on the out skirts of the City. The streets in the immediate vicinity were unpaved; the houses for the most part, were frame buildings. At a much more recent date, when I first entered upon my pastoral duties here, now twenty-seven years since, the old gloomy walls of the Prison, cast their shadows round about. But how is it now? The prison walls have given place to a square of elegant mansions. In the west, you see the Athenæum, towering in tall and grand proportions. In close proximity North, a pile of stately law buildings has been erected. Within a square or so, stand the Court Houses, Custom House, Post Office, and Exchange. Need I speak of the enhanced value of this property. It is patent to all. Our predecessors, in selecting this spot, may be compared to a prudent and noble-hearted man, who, places an inconsiderable amount at interest, to accumulate for after generations. The present value is now, at least, five-fold more than the first investment. And it is evidently for a wise and good purpose. Divine Providence never blesses us with superior gifts, of any kind, to be buried, or, merely to minister to our personal ease and pleasure; but, to be used for the advancement of his cause in our day and generation, and for the good of those who shall come after us. Here then is a capital—judiciously managed—which will enable you at some favorable period in the future, either to erect or purchase a commodious house of worship in some other locality, more convenient to the people than the present one, have a home for the aged poor of the church, and besides, a surplus at interest, sufficient to sustain the Parish, respectably. When this work is accomplished, you will then be in a condition to go vigorously forward to the help of the Lord against the mighty, not only here, but in other, and more destitute places. And may God, in his own good time, usher in that glorious day.

APPENDIX.

OUTLINE SKETCH OF THE BUILDING.

The Church Edifice of St. Thomas, is situated at the S. W. corner of Fifth and Adelphi streets. Its front is on Fifth street. It is a substantial brick building, 40 feet in width, and 60 feet in length—height in proportion.

Its entrance is by a flight of seven marble steps extending north and south, nine feet.

The present style of the Church in its interior, is widely different from the former. The Pulpit and Reading Desk formerly stood at the north side of the building.

A sounding board was then seen suspended from the ceiling over the Pulpit, similar to the one still remaining it St. Peter's Church of this city.

The Orchestra was on the south side, connected with the gallery in the east and west.

The Pews of St. Peter's Church, with their high perpendicular backs, were models from which those of St. Thomas' were constructed.

There were two aisles running east and west, leading from the front door in the east, to the back door in the west, thence into the church yard.

One third of the Basement was fitted up for a Lecture Room and Sunday School; while the remaining two thirds were rented out for storage.

The floor, in remodeling, was raised 3 feet, making the Lecture Room the same size of the body of the church.

The Pulpit, Reading Desk, and Chancel, now stand in the west; back of which is a recess 14 feet in height, and in width 14 feet, extending west 10 feet. This recess leads into the Vestry Room below—dimensions 10 feet by 10. On the upper line of the recess in front, is an entablature supported by two pilasters and two fluted columns, on the frieze of which, is inscribed in golden letters:—

"HOLINESS BECOMETH THINE HOUSE, O LORD, FOREVER."

The Orchestra now stands in the east, connected with the gallery on the north and south side.

The Pews were all modernized, and made of new materials.

The aisles run in the same direction as before, but admit of no egress as formerly into the church yard.

The altering of the church commenced August 5th, 1839, and was completed December of the same year, at a cost of $3600.

The Vestry, in the mean time, hired a large room in Pear street, between Third and Dock streets, where Divine Worship was regularly celebrated.

The introduction of gas, with fixtures, heaters, painting, glazing, &c., was attended with an additional cost of $719.60. Total, $4.319.60.

LIST OF VESTRYMEN FOR 1834 AND 1835.

1834.

John Bowers, } Wardens.
James Johnson, }
Solomon Clarkson.—Sec.
Anthony Cain,
Francis Petts,
John Matthews,
Peter Richmond,
Thomas Charnock,
John Duffins,
* Clayton Miller,
Abraham Williams,
William Jefferson,
Robt. C. Gordon, Jr.,
James C. Matthews,
Joseph P. Cole,
*James Needham,
Robt. C. Gordon, Sr., Treas.
Robt. B. Ayers,
Willis N. Fowles,
*Joshua Brown.

1835.

John Bowers, } Wardens.
James Johnson, }
Solomon Clarkson—Sec.
Anthony Cain,
Francis Petts,
James Foster, Sr.,
Peter Richmond,
Thomas Charnock, Sr.,
John Duffins,
*Clayton Miller,
Abraham Williams,
*Scipio Sewell,
John Matthews,
Robt. C. Gordon, Sr., Treas.
*Josh. Brown,
Frederick A. Hinton,
Ezekiel Sulivan,
Robt. B. Ayers,
Saml. C. Hutchins,
John Allen.

Cato Collins—Clerk.

CERTIFICATE OF CONSECRATION.

"The Rector, Wardens, and Vestrymen of St. Thomas's Church, Philadelphia, Philadelphia county, Pennsylvania, having requested me to consecrate and set apart the House of Worship, lately repaired, and renewed, in, and for, said Parish—

---

* All dead, except those marked with an asterisk.

Be it known, that on this 20th day of December, in the year of our Lord, one thousand eight hundred and thirty-nine, with the rites and solemnities prescribed, I have consecrated and set apart the said House of worship; separating it henceforth from all unhallowed, ordinary and common uses, and dedicating it to the service of the Eternal God, for reading His holy word, for celebrating His holy sacraments, for offering to His glorious Majesty, the sacrifices of prayer and thanksgiving, for blessing His people in His name, and for the performance of all other holy offices, through Jesus Christ, our blessed Lord and Savior, and according to the rites and worship of the Protestant Episcopal Church, in the United States of America.

In testimony whereof, I have hereunto set my hand and seal, and delivered this instrument at Philadelphia, this said 20th day of December, in the year of our Lord, one thousand eight hundred and thirty-nine, and in the thirteenth year of my consecration.

H. U. ONDERDONK,
Bishop of the Prot. Epis. Church in Pennsylvania.

SEASONS OF SPECIAL INTEREST IN SPIRITUAL MATTERS.

The intervening period between the years of 1839, and 1849, was marked with an unusual degree of spiritual interest among the congregation.

We would not, however, be understood as intimating here, that during all this time, no disturbing elements were at work—no ripples upon the sea causing fear of disaster to our little bark in her progress; but, the results for evil were not of so serious a character, as to demand special record. The moral of the whole, was only an additional lesson against the folly of expecting, in this disciplinary state, an unbroken series of either sunshine or clouds.

But as aforesaid, the greater portion of this decade was characterized by the turning of a goodly number from the paths of guilt, shame, and folly, into the ways of wisdom, righteousness, and peace. The Spirit of the Lord, breathed upon the dry bones, disposing many to stand up, go forward to the standard, and enlist under the banner of Christ, to fight against sin, the world, the flesh and Satan. Some of them are still with us manfully struggling against the powers of darkness; a few have halted by the way-side, while a large number of them have been conveyed, we trust, to the Paradise of God, joyfully waiting for the realization of the opening glories of the resurrection morning.

In reviewing the list of Confirmations in those years spoken of, we find a far greater number recorded, than we have for the same space of time that preceded them.

In the year 1840, there were 17 persons confirmed—in 1841, 11—in 1842, 24—in 1843, 21—in 1844, 11—in 1846, 11—in 1848, 10—total, 125.

PETITION TO THE EPISCOPAL CONVENTION IN 1849.

The Vestry of St. Thomas', with the view of having their silence in regard to a certain TEMPORARY regulation, agreed to by their predecessors, no longer construed into passive acquiescence; and desiring the whole responsibility of its continuance—should it be continued—to rest alone upon legislative power and authority; respectfully submitted the following Petition to the Convention of the Protestant Episcopal Church, held in St. Andrew's Church, Philadelphia, May, 1849.

To the Bishop, Clergy, and Laity of the Protestant Episcopal Church in the State of Pennsylvania, in Convention assembled:

The Petition of the Vestry of St. Thomas's African Protestant Episcopal Church, by the Minister and Church Wardens, respectfully represents:—That the aforesaid Church, having been duly organized and constituted a body politic according to the laws of the Commonwealth, and having conformed to the doctrines, discipline, and worship of the Church for more than half a century, to this day stands, unacknowledged, as a branch of the Church in her representative capacity. Your petitioners further represent, that they are fully convinced of the superior adaptedness of our Church to the wants of the people represented by them, and that its having failed to command a more universal acceptance among them, is owing, more than any thing else, to the anomalous and undignified position we occupy, furnishing as it does, ground of no little discontent within, and of much deriding from without. We therefore pray your honorable body to repeal the 8th regulation which prohibits the aforesaid church from being represented in the Convention. All of which is most respectfully submitted to the consideration of your honorable body.

Signed in behalf of the Vestry of St. Thomas's Church, in the city of Philadelphia, May, 1849.

WM. DOUGLASS, *Rector*.

JAMES NEEDHAM,
JNO. L. HART, } *Wardens*

PETITION REFERRED TO A COMMITTEE.

"This Petition was presented by the Rev. Mr. J. Douglass, who submitted the following resolution:

RESOLVED, That the eighth revised regulation of the Convention of the Protestant Episcopal Church in Pennsylvania, be rescinded."

Thursday, May 17th. "Mr. Allibone moved to lay the resolution upon the table, which was carried."

Friday, May 18th. "The Rev. Mr. Montgomery submitted the ensuing resolution, viz.:

RESOLVED, That the petition of the African Church of St. Thomas, to have the eighth revised regulation rescinded, be taken up and referred to a committee of five, with instructions, to report thereupon at the next Convention."

"The Convention proceeded to the consideration of the resolution offered by the Rev. Mr. Montgomery, and it was adopted.

The committee appointed were, the Rev. Messrs. Montgomery, Hare and Breck, and Messrs. G. M. Wharton and T. Wagner."

Philadelphia, May 23d, 1850.
Thursday, 5 o'clock P. M.

"The House proceeded with the special order of the day, fixed for this afternoon, and Mr. G. M. Wharton, from the special committee, on the subject of the African Church, presented the majority "Report," as follows:

"The Special Committee, to whom, at the last Convention, was referred the Petition of the African Church of St. Thomas, to have the Eighth Revised Regulation of this Convention rescinded, beg leave to Report—

The Eighth Revised Regulation was adopted in June, 1795, and declares, that the African Church of St. Thomas, is not entitled to send a Clergyman or Deputies to the Convention, or to interfere with the general government of the Church—this condition having been made, as is recited, in consideration of the peculiar circumstances of such Church at that period—and in 1843 it was further declared by the Convention, that no Church in this Diocese, in like peculiar circumstances with the African Church of St. Thomas, shall be entitled to send a Clergyman or Deputies to the Convention, or to interfere with the general government of the Church.

It appears that about two years before A. D. 1795, the Church of St. Thomas was organized by certain residents of the City of Philadelphia, who were Africans, or descendants of Africans, and were either members or attached to the doctrines and discipline of the Church; and who, moreover, desired to worship God in accordance with her forms and ceremonies, and to submit themselves, as a congregation to the Ecclesiastical Authority of the Diocese. They seem to have been recognized by the Standing Committee and Council of Advice, and, perhaps, by the Convention, as a regular congregation: and had it not been for "peculiar circumstances," would doubtless have been placed on the same footing with the other congregations of our Church. The members of St. Thomas's were desirous of having one of their own color to minister among them, and made application to the Bishop and Standing Committee for their approval of the selection of Absalom Jones, a black man, as their Clergyman, and solicited his ordination—at the same time, requesting a dispensation in his case, from certain literary qualifications enjoined by Canon as prerequisites. The matter was brought before the Convention of the Diocese, and that body agreed to the dispensation which had been requested, and to the recommendation of Mr. Jones for Holy Orders; but, together with a resolution to that effect, passed as a proviso, what is now denominated the Eighth Revised Regulation. The Vestry of St. Thomas's Church, by a formal act, assented to the restriction—and some other stipulations prescribed by the Bishop and Standing Committee being acceded to, Absalom Jones was ordained, and became the settled minister of that Church.

It may be remarked, that this arrangement was evidently a compact entered into, with the view, on the part of the African congregation, of securing the ordination of one of their own people; and might fairly be pressed, by those who are disposed to rest their exclusion on technical grounds, as a strong argument for holding the applicants strictly to the terms of the original contract.

The "peculiar circumstances" referred to in the Proviso, are not stated anywhere on the face of the Journal of the Convention. They may be gathered, however, from the records of the Standing Committee, and of the Church in question, and were probably the following: the color and other physical properties of the parties, their political and social condition—their defects of education and cultivation—and their consequent unfitness, from all these causes, for the situation of legislators and rulers in the Church planted in Pennsylvania. This unfitness seems to have been conceded all round; and it does not appear, that in recognizing and acting upon it, it occurred to our first Diocesan, or to any of the Clergy or Laity who acted with him in the exclusion of the members of St. Thomas's congregation, from a participation in the general government of the Church, that they were violating any principle of that divinely constituted body which they were so earnestly labouring to extend.

It may be, that another circumstance, thought to be "peculiar" in this particular congregation, was the fact, that its Constitution excluded all persons but Africans, and the descendants of Africans, from membership or from holding office therein. There was an exception made, with respect to the rector or minister. This exclusive feature in their organization as a parish, no doubt constitutes a distinction between it and any other in the Diocese, known to the undersigned—and would furnish a plausible argument for refusing to its delegates a seat in this legislative body, all of whose other members represent parishes whose Charters or Articles of Association do not profess to confine membership to any particular tribe of mankind. The Committee, however, are not disposed to place their conclusions upon any narrow basis—particularly one which would not be applicable to other colored congregations adopting a form of Charter similar to that usually selected by our parishes.

The main ground on which the repeal of the Regulation is placed by the advocates of that measure, seems to be, that its continuance is a violation of Christian kindness and courtesy—that it deprives the colored race of a portion of their spiritual privileges, and is an infringement of their inherent right as Christians to participate in the government of the Church. The Committee, on the other hand, regard the Regulation as but the exercise of a clear power of so framing the lay representation of the Church as most to conduce to its general good—as having no concern with the spiritual privileges of the members of Christ's Church—and as founded upon a recognition of the manifest truth, that participation in the legislative power of the Church is but a qualified, and not an absolute right.

In matters of government, where the good of numbers is concerned, and where not individuals, but the public, are chiefly regarded, there can be no violation of courtesy or kindness in withholding what may be thought of particular advantage to some persons, if its concession may prove generally detrimental. The representatives of a community have, in such a case, no right to yield to personal considerations what a stern regard for the common welfare may demand to be retained—and are not invested with that wide discretion in the exercise of their charities or feelings, which may safely be conceded to individuals. If the circumstances of our condition, social and political, are such as to render the change desired by the petitioners a disastrous, or even a dangerous one, every wise and reflecting man will pause, before he permits himself, as a legislator, to be swayed by mere appeals to his sympathies, while his reason and his judgment remain unconvinced.

It is freely admitted, that no considerations of mere expediency can legitimately be weighed in the discussion of a question of right, or can be used as an argument for the violation of the least even of the high and awful privileges which appertain to all the members of the Christian flock. The great point, however, in this matter, which the advocates of the petition are bound to maintain, and which they have entirely failed to demonstrate, is, that the right to a seat in this Convention, as the representative body of the Church in Pennsylvania, and as the Convocation of her Clergy, is any one of the spiritual privileges, which, by baptism or ordination, as the case may be, have been conferred upon her members. Those spiritual privileges which flow from being children of God, members of Christ, and inheritors of the Kingdom of Heaven, are, fortunately, neither conferred nor increased by membership in this body—nor can they be impaired or hindered by absence or exclusion from it. They do not depend upon the arrangements or the votes of men—they are of divine appointment and regulation—existed long before representative Conventions, such as the present, originated—are the individual immunities and comforts of the faithful, without distinction of color, sex, age or nation; and are to be found as untrammelled and unimpaired among the worthy members of the African Church of St. Thomas, as among those of any of the Parishes in union with us. The sanctified water of baptism; the laying on of the Bishop's hands in the Apostolic Rite of Confirmation; and the Holy Communion of the Body and Blood of their crucified Lord; are the Charters of their spiritual privileges, to which the darkest of the children of Africa among us, may point with as high a confidence, and as bright a hope, as any of their white brethren.

The Committee suppose it to be held by all Churchmen, that the constitution of the Christian Church is not of human invention, but of divine origin; and is founded upon the plenary grant of power by the Saviour to his chosen Disciples. They believe that in discharging their high commission, those holy men were guided in their work by the inspiration of the Spirit of God. The Apostles seem to have laid down no fixed form as the only model of a Council of the Church, for want of an exact conformity to which, the proceedings of any attempted Synod are to be considered void. The distinct features of Apostles, Elders and Brethren are clearly developed—and as clearly, the higher prerogative of the Apostles and Elders over the others, in the administration of the affairs of the Church. Doubtless, the inherent power of legislation under the Apostolic Commission, is vested in the chief pastors of the Flock alone; and the joint action of the inferior Clergy, and of the Laity, is invoked and invited by their Bishops, on the ground of mere expediency, and is to be treated as a concession on the part of the latter. This is a ground, however, amply sufficient and certain for all of us, inasmuch as direct Apostolic precedent is furnished for its support.

It appears in the record of the first Council, that St. Paul and Barnabas, and certain others, went up from Antioch to Jerusalem, unto "the Apostles and Elders," about a disputed question, touching the salvation of Gentile converts. It was "the Apostles and Elders who came together to consider of this matter," and the sacred record implies, that "the much disputing" was confined to them; while it distinctly states, that the authoritative judgment was pronounced by one of the Apostolic College. The whole body of the Church, then present in Jerusalem, seem undoubtedly to have been consulted, and to have signified their satisfaction with the sentence promulgated by St. James. And yet it is as undoubted a fact, that the brethren of Antioch, who were directly interested in the question to be decided, were not personally present in the Council at Jerusalem, nor do they seem to have been represented there by delegates forming a constituent portion of that Assembly. The Committee do not perceive in the Scriptural account of this celebrated Synod, any model pattern of a representative assembly of the Church.

Turning to times but a little later, we perceive that a somewhat different Constitution of Church Councils is presented, the right to a seat being apparently confined to the highest order of the Clergy, and the participation of the Laity altogether dispensed with. The long practice of the Christian Church, in perhaps every branch of it, may fairly be considered as demonstrating, that the introduction of laymen into Church government is, by no means, the consequence of any absolute right; and even the practice of our own branch of the Church, which has, beyond all others, the most clearly affirmed the privilege of the Laity to become a component part of her legislative authority, as conclusively proves this right to be the subject of condition and regulation. Witness our positive Canon Law, which has limited the number of lay deputies, and prescribed their qualifications as worshippers in the parish which they may represent—and indeed, treats the whole subject as one altogether within the discretionary control of the Church herself.

So, too, with regard to the body of the Clergy.

Their participation in Church government seems to have been equally under regulation with that of their Lay brethren. In those early Councils which our Church has always regarded as œcumenical, and whose acts she has consequently recognized as authoritative, the Bishops alone took their seats. The Canon of the Great Council of Nice, as well as the Apostolic Canon which provides for the assembling of Councils and Synods, as a means of preserving unity and peace, required *the Bishops* of the Province to meet together and settle the ecclesiastical controversies which might have occurred. If we turn to our Mother Church of England, which may, by some, be considered the nearest and safest guide for ourselves—(to say nothing of the absolute exclusion of the Laity from her Church Councils proper,) we find that her Convocations consisted but in part of those who sat by virtue of their order; while the others attended as chosen representatives of the body of the Priesthood. And it is perfectly familiar to all of us, that a large portion of our own Clergy, inferior to none of their brethren in learning and experience, full Presbyters, and above all personal exception, arè excluded from a voice and a seat here, under the exercise of a power, which, unless it be lawful, is uncatholic, grossly despotic and unjust.

If the considerations which the Committee have presented, be well founded, the admission or rejection of the Clergymen and deputies from the African Church—and the throwing open of the doors of this Convention to others similarly circumstanced, becomes a question of mere expediency, to be decided according to each one's views of the edifying or hurtful consequences of the act. Our legislation should be for the good of the Church, and to secure, so far as our judgments can do so, her prosperity and advancement. And let us ask, can there be a doubt, with dispassionate persons, as to the incompetency of the parties in question, for the post of advisers and legislators in the concerns of this portion of the American Church? Are they qualified for it, either by education, cultivation, or social position? Would their decisions and acts carry with them aught of the moral influence which is so desirable an attendant upon the decrees of authority? Are members of this House fully and sincerely prepared to receive the proposed new comers in such way as to exhibit in nothing, a distinction between them and others on the floor; and are they not fearful of betraying, in even the slightest degree, a feeling indicative of the absence of that entire equality and confraternity, which should mark the intercourse of the members of such an assemblage as this? Is there no reason to apprehend that heart-burning or jealousy will spring up from imagined, perhaps actual slights, induced by the unconquerable aversion, in many, to the admixture of races physically so diverse and separate, as the black and the white? Gentlemen must answer these questions, and many more such, satisfactorily, before they can grant the prayer of the Petition.

It is believed that the agitation of this proposal

would not have arisen from the spontaneous action of the parties themselves, and that there is no general, natural feeling among them, of supposed wrong or oppression. For more than half a century, the Church in Pennsylvania has been at rest on this point—quietly pursuing her way, undisturbed by the contests which have had their rise in the unfortunate infusion into our population, of the children of Africa. Providence, ages ago, had planted them in another quarter of the globe; in one perhaps specially designed for their inhabitation. It is not known to the Committee, that the voluntary migration of these tribes from their original seats has ever darkened the shores of other lands—but the hands of cruel and mercenary men tore them unwillingly from their homes, and more genial clime, and rudely transferred them to a distant Continent, there to grow and to multiply as the mere bondmen and serfs of another race. Their position with us may well be considered as an *error loci*—and the retributive justice of the Almighty, for the inceptive wrong of their original subjection, seems to have travelled with them as a moral plague, and to have rendered their presence the constant source of disturbance and evil. Far be it from the Committee to undervalue the sufferings of this portion of their fellow-men, to extenuate the wrongs done to them, or to add a feather's weight to the depression resting upon them. On the contrary, they are earnest to recognize, in the fullest extent, the obligation upon the whites to exert, in behalf of their colored brethren, the broadest extent of protection and comfort—to regard them as in a state of tutelage, and as especially committed by a common Father, to their kindness and consideration, and particularly do they feel the duty of being actuated in all their dealings with them, by the most large-hearted charity. But they consider it a most signal error, to break down every barrier which instinctive nature has reared in the path of free intercourse; and they are of opinion, that the misjudged, though well meant effort to place them on this floor, will conduce to their eventual injury.

The Committee deprecate now, and in the future, the agitation of this question. We all know how sensitive the public mind is, throughout every part of our wide country, with respect to the colored race; and we see no prospect of this sensitiveness being eradicated. The main topic has fearfully convulsed the political union of our Republic, and has broken the bonds which had previously connected some denominations of Christians. Our branch of the Church has thus far been protected from any considerable excitement upon this head—yet it requires but a moderate share of sagacity to perceive, how the pushing of the proposed change to its legitimate results may endanger the permanence of our ecclesiastical organization as an American Church of United Dioceses. Fortunately, the Divine Constitution of the Body of Christ preserves the essential unity of that holy fellowship, in spite of every merely social convulsion. And yet no true friend of the Church, but would regret the rude sundering of those ties of outward communion, which conduce so materially to the influence and the dignity of the spiritual body itself. Serious indeed seems the responsibility of commencing a series of measures which may tend to such disastrous consequences; and the Committee, therefore, would gladly see this whole matter laid permanently and quietly at rest, by a decided and expressive vote of the Convention, where fifty years of universal acquiescence has placed it. Gladly would they see the wise arrangement, sanctioned by the prudent apprehension of Bishop White and his coadjutors in the work of framing our ecclesiastical Constitution, continue unbroken and undisturbed; and they accordingly submit the following Resolution as expressive of their views.

Resolved, That it is inexpedient to repeal the Eighth Revised Regulation, and that the Committee be discharged from the further consideration of the subject.

G. M. WHARTON,
CHAS. BRECK,
TOBIAS WAGNER,
Committee."

Phila., *May* 21, A.D. 1850.

MINORITY REPORT ON PETITION IN 1850.

"The undersigned, a minority of the Committee appointed at the last Convention of the Diocese, to consider the petition of the church of St. Thomas in this city, for the repeal of the eighth revised regulation, report, that in their opinion, the manner and matter of the petition entitle it to serious and respectful consideration.

It appears from the records of St. Thomas's Church, (though the minutes of the standing committee do not show it, which however about the time refused to bear evidence, being very imperfect) that at a meeting of the standing committee and Council of Advice, of this Diocese, held September 9th, 1794, "the Rt. Rev. Bishop White laid before the Council, the Constitution of the African Church of St. Thomas, a congregation of the people of color, who having lately erected a building for the public worship of God, do now, in consequence of free and mature deliberation, propose and request to be associated with the Protestant Episcopal Church in the United States, and, in particular, to commit all their ecclesiastical affairs to the rule and authority of the Bishop and Church in this State."

The Bishop and Council, being pleased with the above application, and willing to accept the terms "therein," it was RESOLVED, and declared therefore, that, as soon as the Trustees or Deputies of the said congregation, being duly authorized, shall sign the Act of Association of the Church in this State, they shall be entitled to all the privileges of the other congregations of the Protestant Episcopal Church; agreed, that Dr. Samuel Magaw and Dr. Robert Blackwell, be a Committee to meet the Trustees or Deputies of the African Church, and see them ratify the Act of Association.

(Signed,) SAMUEL MAGAW,
A member of the Council.

It appears also, from the records referred to, that, at a meeting of the Standing Committee, held Oct. 23d, 1794, an address or letter to the Bishop and Clergy of the Protestant Episcopal Church in Philadelphia, from the Trustees and other Representatives of the Congregation of the African Church, now called St. Thomas's Church, of Philadelphia, was laid before the Council, communicated through the hands of the Bishop, representing, among other things, that it would be expedient to have among themselves a pious and duly qualified man of color, to discharge the functions of a minister, and recommending for the said purpose as a candidate, Absalom Jones, a man of good report and godly conversation.

Whereupon, the Council being heartily disposed to favor the address and application as above, and entirely satisfied, as far as doth to them appear, of the moral and religious character of the person recommended, do agree in opinion and respectfully advise, that the most regular mode of proceeding, is for the Bishop to give his sanction and approbation to Absalom Jones, to officiate as a reader of Divine Service, &c., in the said Church, and a candidate for Deacon's Orders, till the meeting of the Convention of the Church in this State; the 7th Canon, ratified in General Convention, requiring with regard to learning of those who are to be ordained, "That the requisition of an acquaintance with Latin and Greek, is only to be dispensed with by two-thirds of the Convention of the State to which the candidate belongs, and for good causes moving thereto."

Now in the former part of this "address and application" laid before the Standing Committee, and received by them with favor, occur the following statements—"On Tuesday, August 12th, 1794, at a special meeting held for the purpose, the Constitution of our Church was unanimously ratified upon the principles of the Protestant Episcopal Church of North America, and on application to the Bishop and Clergy of the Protestant Episcopal Church of Philadelphia, we were graciously received into the bosom of the Church, and on Sunday, September 14th, 1794, the Bishop in public did receive us under his pastoral charge, and on Sunday, October 12th, 1794, our being received into the fellowship and communion of the Protestant Episcopal Church of Philadelphia, was most cordially and fully announced from the pulpit by the Rev. Rob't. Blackwell."

It appears, therefore, most clearly, from these records, that, at this time, September, 1794, St. Thomas's Church was entitled to all the privileges of the other Protestant Episcopal congregations in the Diocese, among which was the right of sending Deputies to the State Convention. The Act of Association "done in Christ Church," in this city, the "24th day of May, 1785," expressly providing that the clergy and congregations duly ratifying the said act, shall be called and known by the name of the Protestant Episcopal Church in the State of Pennsylvania, and that each congregation may send to the Convention a Deputy or Deputies, and that all such clergymen as shall hereafter be settled as the ministers of the congregations ratifying this act, shall have the same privileges, and be subject to the same regulations as the clergy now subscribing the same."

Thus stood the matter in September, 1794, when, as the undersigned believe, St. Thomas's Church was in full fellowship with the Church, and entitled to all the privileges of the other congregations of the Protestant Episcopal Church in the Diocese.

In the Convention of the succeeding year (June 2nd, 1795,) "It was moved and seconded, that in the examination for Holy Orders of Absalom Jones, a black man, belonging to the African Church of St. Thomas, in this city, the knowledge of the Latin and Greek languages be dispensed with, agreeably to the Canon.

RESOLVED, That the same be granted, provided it is not to be understood to entitle the African Church to send a clergyman or Deputies to the Convention, or to interfere with the general government of the Episcopal Church, this condition being made, in consideration of their peculiar circumstances at present."

On Wednesday, August 12th, 1795, at a meeting of the Trustees of St. Thomas's Church, the Rt. Rev. Bishop and several of the Clergy of the Diocese being present, the Bishop presented the above extract from the Journal of the Convention, which was "read and explained, and the members present, uniting with the restrictions therein specified, it was agreed to."

The undersigned, therefore, while granting the

Trustees of St. Thomas's Church did agree to the restrictions referred to, cannot see why such assent should prevent the present authorities of that Church from seeking the removal of a provision which the congregation have found by experience to be burdensome and injurious to their interests. The said restriction was imposed and agreed to, let it be remembered, not according to the records cited, at the time of receiving the Church of St. Thomas into fellowship with the Church in the Diocese, but nearly a year afterwards, when the question of the dispensation of certain literary qualifications in the person selected for their minister came before the Convention, "this condition being made in consideration of their peculiar circumstances at present."

The restriction and the agreement to it are therefore, in the opinion of the undersigned, not to be viewed in the light of an original compact contemporaneous with the existence of the Church of St. Thomas as a part of the Church in the Diocese. The agreement they yielded to the restriction in their peculiar exigency, by no means interferes with the right of the congregation to petition now for a repeal of the prohibition which their present "peculiar circumstances" may render highly oppressive, and detrimental to their prosperity.

But what were the "peculiar circumstances" to which the restriction, passed in 1795, refers? The words "at present" ought, in charity, to be strictly limited. The Reverend Absalom Jones, the first minister of St. Thomas's Church, though very deficient in literary qualifications for the ministry, was a "man of good report and godly conversation." He was held in great reverence and esteem by the colored people of our city. Zealous for the prosperity of the Church, and unwearied in doing good, he was especially beloved in consequence of his devotion to the sick and dying at the time of the prevalence of that awful scourge, the yellow fever. Administering to the bodily as well as spiritual wants of many poor sufferers, and soothing the last moments of many departing souls among his people, he became greatly endeared to the colored race.

Hence, when they formed a congregation, in order that they might worship God according to the doctrine and discipline of the Church of their choice, they fixed their hearts upon having their kind friend and helper for their minister. He who had already won his way to their hearts by labors and sacrifices of Christian love that no one can hear of without emotion, must be the shepherd of their souls in Christ Jesus. So that they could succeed in this their darling wish, they were content to submit to inconvenience and to loss; for him their friend and brother, bound so closely to their hearts by the sympathy of past afflictions, they were ready to be placed for the time being in a position of inferiority,

They were fully sensible that he did not possess the literary qualifications requisite for the ministry, but they knew and loved his self-sacrificing spirit, and consistently religious life. When, therefore, the great difficulty in the way of his ordination was removed, by the dispensing vote of the convention, the condition on which, in this case, the dispensation depended was agreed to, the congregation of St. Thomas had succeeded in their great desire. In their feebleness, they surrendered to the far stronger power, the right which the church had already given them, in order that their little flock might be watched and ministered to by a shepherd whom they loved.

The undersigned earnestly submit, whether, after the expiration of so many years, advantage should be taken of the concession which the petitioners yielded in their then peculiar exigency? More than half a century has passed away since the adoption of the restriction, which, they now respectfully ask, may be removed. Their present Pastor has, it is believed, far superior literary qualifications to the Rev. Absalom Jones, having passed a very creditable examination, for the Diaconate and Priesthood, before the Rt. Rev. Bishop Onderdonk, of this city.

The very wording of the restriction referred to, viewed in connexion with the facts above stated, shows that both parties, the Convention on the one hand and the Trustees of St. Thomas's Church on the other, thought of it only as a temporary proviso, and that it would be rescinded when the "peculiar circumstances" spoken of should cease.

It is believed by the undersigned, that the "peculiar circumstances" of the church of the petitioners at that time have in a great measure changed; that special peculiarity aimed at in the restriction has ceased, from the fact above stated, with regard to the present minister of the parish, and also from the consideration that their congregation are suffering a reproach now which they did not experience at the time the restriction was agreed to, being contrasted unfavorably with a colored Presbyterian congregation, whose minister had a seat in the Presbytery. The undersigned submit, that, even on these accounts, the restriction should be immediately rescinded.

But some may contend that St. Thomas's Church is not, and never has been, in union with the Convention in the Diocese. The undersigned cannot permit themselves to doubt that it has been duly received, and that, too, at a very early day, into the communion and fellowship of the Church, as the records of the Parish and the facts of the case furnish strong evidence of it. But grant, for the sake of argument, that it has not been admitted as a part of the Church of the Diocese. The supposition is favored, it must be confessed, by the fact that the journals for several successive years before 1832, after a list of the congregations in the State, append these words: "There is, also, in Philadelphia, St. Thomas's African Church, not in union with this Convention." Granting, we say, that this is the fact, though the undersigned think it far otherwise, then it may well be asked, where is the necessity of a restriction so calculated to wound the feelings of those concerned?

According to this supposition, the danger of St.

Thomas's Church sharing in the legislation of the Church is effectually guarded against already. They do not yet possess, by right of communion and fellowship with the Church, the privilege which it is the object of the Eighth Revised Regulation to take away. If not in union with us, they cannot send their representatives among us, until, by an express vote of the Convention, we admit them to such union. In this view, the restriction is entirely useless—a gratuitous insult to the persons who are the subjects of it. Even the strongest opponents to the admission of the representatives of St. Thomas's Church may, if the said Church be not in union with us, vote for the repeal of the regulation as superfluous and objectionable.

The undersigned submit, that the Eighth Revised Regulation be rescinded on principle. No test of admission should be adopted here which is at variance with the precepts of our Redeemer, and with the practice of the Church in the apostolic times,—and the undersigned would ask whether the said regulation be not inconsistent with both? If it be urged that darkness of the skin is just cause for exclusion, let us look well at such passages as these from the blessed Gospel: "One is your Master, even Christ; and all ye are brethren." "God hath made of one blood all nations of men, for to dwell on all the face of the earth." And by His own blood, shed once for all men, hath Christ "redeemed us to God out of every kindred, and tongue, and people, and nation." There is no color marked out by our Divine Master and Head for exclusion from even the smallest privilege or honor of the Christian Church. On the contrary, it is part of the glory of the Church, "that God is no respecter of persons," but that all are equally the objects of His parental care and His redeeming love.

At the first Council of the Church, after our Lord's ascension, "the apostles, elders and brethren were assembled with one accord." It will not be contended that any exception was then and there taken to the hue of the complexion. But it is alleged that the exclusion of the Church of St. Thomas, and all others "in like peculiar circumstances," is a mere matter of expediency, and is not at all connected with the spiritual privileges of our excluded brethren: that the regulation as to who shall or shall not sit in council with us is a subject pertaining *only* to the legislative character of the Church.

Without considering the great inconsistency of the legislative affairs being governed by any rules that seem at variance with the precepts and spirit of Christianity, we think that the above allegation will lose even its plausibility, when it is considered that the exclusion of this Church from our councils does interfere indirectly with spiritual privileges of the petitioners. The Parish in question is cut off from what is certainly to be considered a privilege and an honor, the conferring with a band of brothers about the welfare of the Church, and aiding in the promotion of such plans and regulations as may seem best adapted to advance the cause of our beloved Redeemer.

The singularity of its long exclusion, and the stamp of inferiority which is thereby put upon it, are well calculated, as the congregation respectfully set forth in their petition, "to furnish ground of no little discontent within, and of constant deriding from without." Hence they are hindered from greater progress as a congregation, and a subject of vexation and reproach is constantly kept before them.

It may well be asked if it be consistent with the declaration of the great Apostle to the Gentiles, "if meat make my brother to offend, I will eat no flesh while the world standeth, lest I make my brother to offend," thus to wound the feelings and to interfere with the peace and prosperity of a company of our brethren. They cannot be expected long to reconcile the inconsistency of their pastor being fit to preach the word of God, and to administer His Holy Sacraments, and yet incapable of having any part in the councils of the Church. Can we reasonably look for their advancement and improvement in knowledge and virtue, while we continue to give ground for attacks upon their position, and thus help to lessen their self-respect.

It seems, also, to the undersigned, well worthy of consideration, whether the repeal of the Eighth Revised Regulation would not tend to produce peace in our own Convention?

It is believed that many of the members of this body are conscientiously opposed to it. It is an offence to them, and they would rejoice to see it rescinded. While it remains on the statute book, it will tend to provoke agitation and dispute, not only on account of its exclusive nature, but also from its remarkable singularity. In no part of the Church, it is believed, is a similar prohibition maintained with such invidious prominence.

In conclusion, the undersigned seek, by God's grace, to free our Church in this Diocese from what, they have reason to believe, affords ground with many, without, for the charge against us of inconsistency.

They solemnly disclaim any purpose, or even wish, to involve this question with subjects of an exciting nature, that have no legitimate connexion. They desire to have the subject discussed, and entreat that it may be so discussed, on its own merits alone, without being embarrassed and perplexed with topics that properly have nothing at all to do with it, and with which the undersigned have not the slightest intention to interfere.

They present the following resolution: "That the Eighth Revised Regulation be and is hereby rescinded."

All which is respectfully submitted.

HENRY E. MONTGOMERY.

PHILADA., May 21, 1850.

The subscriber agrees cordially with the main principles of the above report.

G. EMLEN HARE.

RESOLUTION REPORTED BY MAJORITY COMMITTEE ADOPTED.

" The Convention proceeded to the consideration of the resolution submitted by the majority of the special committee on the subject of the Eighth Revised Regulation. The vote was called for by ayes and noes, and by orders, and stood as follows:

CLERGY.	LAY REPRESENTATIONS—CHURCHES.	
Ayes—44.	Ayes—51.	
Noes—42.	Noes—16.	Divided—1.

"So the resolution reported by the 'majority' committee was adopted. The Convention then adjourned."

EXPRESSION OF SENTIMENT

From the Vestry of St. Thomas's Protestant Episcopal Church, in relation to the action of the Episcopal Convention of the Diocese of Pennsylvania, on the majority report of a committee to whom was referred a certain petition from the aforesaid Church, respectfully asking a repeal of the Eighth Revised Regulation.

At an adjourned meeting of the Vestry of St. Thomas's Protestant Episcopal Church, held Monday evening, June 3d, 1850, the following preamble and resolutions reported by a committe previously appointed, were accepted and unanimously adopted. The said committee were also authorized to publish the same in such papers as they might deem proper to select.

WHEREAS, The Minister, Church Wardens and Vestrymen of St. Thomas's Protestant Episcopal Church, did send in a petition to the Episcopal Convention of the Diocese of Pennsylvania, sitting in Philadelphia, May, 1849, praying said Convention to repeal the Eighth Regulation, which prohibits the aforesaid Church from being represented by delegation, having been under the superintendence of the Bishop of the Diocese upwards of fifty-five years; and having conformed to the doctrines, discipline and worship of the Episcopal Church during the period above mentioned; AND WHEREAS, the said petition was referred to a committee of five gentlemen to report to the Convention to be held at St. Andrew's Church in 1850; and whereas, a majority of the committee not only reported adversely to the prayer of the petitioners, but betrayed a spirit very unbecoming professing Christians, announcing in their report that our "COLOR, PHYSICAL AND SOCIAL CONDITION AND EDUCATION, RENDERING US ENTIRELY UNFIT TO SIT IN DELIBERATIVE BODIES;" and whereas, we are not surprised at the final result, yet we confess that we are perfectly astounded to find that it was thought necessary in so solemn an assembly, in order to reach the result, to condescend to appeal to those unrighteous prejudices unknown in the Constitution of the Church, and the Book of Common Prayer, and utterly at variance with all the principles, precepts and doctrines, as laid down by the great Head of the Church:

Therefore, Resolved, That if we were heretofore

desirous of being admitted into union with the Convention, we are not now, nor can we hereafter be, (with due respect to ourselves and posterity) while "COLOR, PHYSICAL AND SOCIAL CONDITION AND EDUCATION," continue to be the test of admission or rejection.

Resolved, As the sense of this Vestry, that the members of St. Thomas's Church have common understanding, and know how to appreciate virtue, honesty and industry, as well as other people, let their complexion be what it may.

Resolved. That in the opinon of this Vestry, the expressions that were used by some of the members of the Convention, should be kept from the heathen, lest the Gospel should fail to have its salutary effect upon their minds, they instinctively rejecting the message at the hands of those who justify complexional distinctions in the Church of Christ.

Resolved. That expediency is no plea against the violation of the great principles of charity, mercy, justice, and truth.

Resolved. That the consideration offered, by reminding us that the rejection could not debar us from communion with the Spirit, did not, in our humble opinion, come with very good grace, after having been told, in terms not to be misunderstood, that we were "entirely unfit" to hold visible fellowship with a delegated council of that body, which defines the Church to be a "VISIBLE BODY of faithful men," &c., whose high mission on earth is fulfilled only so far as she is a co-worker with the Spirit.

Resolved. That the thanks of this Vestry be, and are hereby tendered to that portion of the Convention, who endorsed by their votes the minority report, which developes the true Catholic spirit, beautifully harmonizing with all that is pure, holy and elevating in the Christian system.

JAMES NEEDHAM,
CLAYTON MIDLER,
J. C. BOWERS,
J. L. HART,
FRANKLIN TURNER.
} *Committee.*

PETITION OF ST. THOMAS'S CHURCH IN 1854.

A petition from the Vestry of St. Thomas's Church, containing the same request of the former one, signed by the Rev. Wm. Douglass, and James Needham, Warden, was forwarded to the Episcopal Convention, assembled in St. Andrew's Church, May, 1854. This petition was presented on Wednesday, May 17th, by the Rev. Mr. Spackman, who "then gave notice that on Thursday he would move to repeal the Eighth Revised Regulation."

"Thursday afternoon 5 P. M. The Convention re-assembled. The minutes of the morning session were read and approved.

"The Rev. Dr. Clay withdrew his motion to lay the resolution of the Rev. Mr. Spackman, offered this morning, on the table. The vote was then taken by Orders on Mr. Spackman's resolution to repeal the Eighth Revised Regulation, as follows:

CLERGY.		LAITY.	
Ayes, . .	70	Ayes, . .	32
Noes, . .	28	Noes, . .	40

One divided.

" So the resolution was lost."

LIST OF THE PRESENT VESTRY.

Clayton Miller,	James Needham, } Wardens.
Joshua Brown—Treas.,	Scipio Sewell, }
John C. Bowers,—Sec.,	William H. Riley,
Morris Brown—Clerk,	Edward W. Venning,
Ulysses B. Vidal,	Thomas Charnock,
Edward Collins,	James H. George,
James S. Douglass,	William P. Price,
Hamilton D. Wilson,	William Knight,
Franklin Turner,	Geo. T. Burrell,
James H. Wilson, M. D.	Joseph H. Carter.

In 1849, a brick wall was erected, in extent 175 feet, forming the letter L, 8 feet high from the pavement, 13 inches thick, enclosing the church yard at a cost of $470.

In 1859, an Organ, which had not been long in use—of much greater volume than the former one, was purchased—value, $1200.

The principal debt of the church at this date, (1861) is a balance due on the Organ of about $175.

CONFIRMATIONS, BAPTISMS, &c.

Confirmations from 1834 to 1860,		272,
Baptisms—Infants, . .	163	
" Adults, . .	42	
Total	205	
Communicants—present number,		105.
Congregation " " more or less,		337.
Sunday School—number of pupils—Male,		47.
" " " " " Female,		58.
Teachers—Male, ...		5.
" Female		13.

SOCIETIES.

Children's Aid Society.
Sinking Fund Society.

The Sinking Fund Society of St. Thomas's Church superintend its cleansing at proper seasons, and aid in meeting other incidental expenses, not otherwise provided for.

The funds of the Children's Aid Society are applied to furnishing clothing to the children of such parents, whose only plea for not sending them to Sunday School, is their want of decent apparel. Both these societies are composed chiefly of females. And, I cannot feel that my task is completed, without recording, as I now do, my high estimate,—ever to be cherished—of "their works and labor of love which they have showed for Christ's sake." May Heaven's choicest benedictions rest upon them.

THE END.

www.ingramcontent.com/pod-product-compliance
Lightning Source LLC
LaVergne TN
LVHW011237110826
845150LV00006B/1658